D1460028

March 8, 2017

For Adrienne,

DEEP SALT WATER

I hope you wade in the ocean soon, let you finally feel the water...

MARIANNE APOSTOLIDES

DEEP
SALT
WATER

MIXED MEDIA COLLAGE BY
CATHERINE MELLINGER

BookThug • 2017

FIRST EDITION

Copyright © 2017 by Marianne Apostolides
Mixed Media Collage © 2017 by Catherine Mellinger

ALL RIGHTS RESERVED

No part of this publication may be reproduced or transmitted in any form or by any means, electronic or mechanical, including photocopying, recording, or any information storage or retrieval system, without permission in writing from the publisher.

The production of this book was made possible through the generous assistance of the Canada Council for the Arts and the Ontario Arts Council. BookThug also acknowledges the support of the Government of Canada through the Canada Book Fund and the Government of Ontario through the Ontario Book Publishing Tax Credit and the Ontario Book Fund.

The author wishes to acknowledge the support of the Ontario Arts Council, through the Writers' Reserve and Writers' Works in Progress programs.

Library and Archives Canada Cataloguing in Publication

Apostolides, Marianne, author
Deep salt water / Marianne Apostolides ; Catherine Mellinger, artist.
-- First edition.

Issued in print and electronic formats.
ISBN 978-1-77166-278-9 (softcover).--ISBN 978-1-77166-279-6 (HTML).--
ISBN 978-1-77166-280-2 (PDF).--ISBN 978-1-77166-281-9 (Kindle)

1. Apostolides, Marianne. 2. Authors, Canadian (English)--21st
century--Biography. I. Mellinger, Catherine, 1980-, illustrator II. Title.

PS8601.P58Z46 2017   C818'.6   C2016-907834-5
                                              C2016-907835-3

Mixed media collages by Catherine Mellinger photographed by Melanie Gordon
Cover image by Catherine Mellinger: Jellyfish, mixed media collage on paper, 2016
Interior images by Catherine Mellinger: She Swims, Scuba, Anemone, Whips, Muscle, Colony, Lungs
2, Seaweed (all) mixed media collage on paper, 2016
The production of these works was made possible by the Region of Waterloo Arts Fund.
All works from the collection of the artist. Used with permission.

Marianne Apostolides author photograph by Melanie Gordon

PRINTED IN CANADA

*To the man who
stands and observes*

CONTENTS

Fetal development during the first trimester is the most active. During the first trimester fetal development has new things arriving every day and week.

#1.

Blythe was a fish in my body. Her eyes are open in the murk. My water broke and the whole sea spilled. It came without warning: the gush of the ocean. A sac of grief floods cities and women. I float like sleep until I'm emptied. Now I'm bone, and the hard-round planet will push to be born.

But I am confusing events.

Her eyes are glaciers: sparkle, ageless, all of time is in her eyes. She weeps, and years dissolve from history. I try to stop her: lick one tear. My lips will wrap around the capsule. It seems, for a time, I can almost forget why I'm sad.

She breathed through her navel he kisses. I like my oranges blood red. We stole avocados and peeled their skins. He fed me lotus like dinosaurs' eggs. We were young and in love. We were careless, in pleasure, but we saw the signs: *two lines equal*—

Flush our waste. The bodies drifted down the water. Who will decide? The decisions are made. We used our tongues. We tipped the balance. Vacuum, suction: how will we dispose of the dead? Lips blink in the murk—there's nothing to breathe. The oxygen only comes from a tube.

Her first cry, when I hear it, is the piercing surprise of living.

#2.

"Mama?"
"Yes, sweetie."

"Why is there seaweed on your body?"
"Because I'm a woman."

"Then I'm not a woman."
"Not yet," I say. But you will be, my love... "Now open wide."

I place a grain of sand in her mouth, tucked deep beneath her tongue.

I was twenty-three when my pearl was formed. He hadn't yet kissed me; I already knew. I'm stubborn and wilful. My mother repeatedly called me a "misery." She wasn't wrong: I was never meant to be a child.

"Next slide, please."

He was giving a keynote. I sat at the back of the conference room. The slide dropped down: projected, bright, he described his findings. I watched his hands; I set my sights. When I awoke in the hotel bed, the jewel was luminous in my mouth.

"Next slide."

I learned from experience: Blythe would get her grain of sand from my clean fingers. This is the duty of the mother. My mom didn't realize; she never put the sand in my mouth. I discovered, by accident. Women were frolicking in the waves. The Greek wore swim trunks the colour of cherries; his mass of hair was matted and wet. It's the scent of the ocean. "He's catching fish with his hands," my mother said. In the rocks, in the shallows, where water is warm. He bent forward, ass high, both his hands submerged. "It doesn't need to be deep," he said. He winked, as if he'd caught me, looking.

"Next slide."

The man sold marble from quarries in Greece. He'd shown us samples, which we all touched. I liked the one with emerald green, with veins of black. He saw me, fondling. He wouldn't tell a soul, he said. Finger to his lips; fingers to my lips. The shower was running. My swimsuit was clammy; it rolled like a tube down my thighs in the water. The man was watching: smiles like cherries. My mother had warned me about the ocean, but he was family. We didn't suspect it. The marble was smooth, with a sheen like liquid. "Rub it," he said. He was panting now. He'd caught a fish. I heard the thrash. It's frantic, with the long-fat muscle in his palm. That night, I found a grain of sand in the folds of my body. I took it, furtive, to my tongue.

"Next slide, please."

This is the power of undertow: not blithe on the shore, with lotion, bikinis; with dry sand and music. That's not denial. That's ignorance, childhood: sun without blisters. But my will is monstrous. I see an octopus moving in water. The bulb of its head is the frightening part. We can feel it approaching: the suckers and tentacles, massive brain. It's jetting forward. I understand fear.

Slide like lava, warm and thickly: undertow.
Three-quarters of all species will be dead.

Her lifetime is ended, a curious thing.

With my head on his chest, I'll convince myself that the worst is
over. Next slide, *"Please!"*: the octopus is moving faster.

#3.

We danced beneath palm trees whose fronds are pink and blue. We dance at the bottom of the ocean. Scuba divers swim in suits, the tanks of nitrous on their backs. "It's his *favourite*," one says as he hands me the hose. My shirt is silver, iridescent. "Coral reefs are *dying*," he adds. But I've never tried it. Flesh and softness, psychedelic. "Now, though, all that's left is *bone*." It seems incongruous. Someone walks by with a stack of towels: creamy white and fluffed with scent.

We laugh as we inhale the nitrous; I notice his eyes beneath the mask. "It's an *orgy*!" he says. (It's Timothy Leary's birthday party.) A woman is dancing. Her hair flows upward: fingers combing wet strands. I suck the nitrous, watch the woman. Sounds pulse like inside a womb. "It's an orgy among the *phytoplankton*!" Ocean plants are eating the minerals poured into rivers. The fertilizers sprayed on crops run through the mouth. She kisses me. My shirt is silver. Radiant toys are washed onto shore.

The man with the nitrous can't stop talking—information, overflow—I listen, but the sounds distort. They rubber and bend. Am I hearing it wrong? We only intended to make ripe tomatoes, then phytoplankton reproduce. "They reproduce and then they *die*!" We burst into laughter. Inhale the oddness: dancers are snatching at the hose. "But then bacteria eat the *dead*." They're gorging themselves. "They swallow the *oxygen*!" Nothing is left in the dead zones but nitrous.

Children gather at Leary's feet like they had in the '60s, but now they're adults with bad knees and bad teeth. *This* is the end of their revolution: consciousness-raising, music thrum, the children toke—but nitrogen rises, making the planet hotter and stranger. I look at the palm trees outside the window; I venture to speak: "We haven't sacrificed enough." Leary stares at me, a steely gaze. "That's easy to say when you're young," he replies. I've entered and disturbed the water. You're standing, observing how currents flow.

We listen to Leary. The ramble bubbles out his mouth. Again, I speak. He interrupts. I ought to be quiet, accept my position: a girl on the floor at the feet of a master. But I'm the one who thrashes, flails. The metal hooks, the mouth gets cut, and I don't care: I'd rather be free and blood in the ocean. '*That's easy to say...*' I leave, mid-sentence—swim off, breast stroke, toward the mermaid. "Hi!" she says. "Have you seen Leary?" "He's giving a lecture..." He's earned it. He's dying. "But so is the *planet!*" the diver retorts.

The dance floor is packed with swaying bodies: forests of sea kelp and sharks between. "They pissed away a gold *opportunity*." Berkeley, now, is safer than Disneyland. "Where's the danger?" "All around us." Suck the nitrous. Sodden, ugly—sounds start bulging—purple-black against my eyes. Stricken, I stop: stock-still on the dance floor. The diver has noticed. He feeds me ecstasy so I feel better. "It's all so sad," I say. He laughs. "Your sadness is beautiful." Kiss his lips, he lifts his mask; his tears cascade on my skin.

I don't love the mermaid, or even the man with the laughing gas. The love flows through, but it won't last: it's manufactured, little pill. Like psychedelic phytoplankton, coral reefs and Leary's brain. I love the man who stands and observes. We met in the starlight when planets were forming. I will not meet him until tomorrow. We'll make a child who won't be born.

I've never come to terms for this. Not yet. You'll see.

#4.

If I were a fish, I'd be a salmon. Leap like fireworks—pinkness and viscera—I like it best when currents are strong. This has built good muscle. But they'll peel my skin: it's too fatty and real. Still, I'll taste quite nice with feta cheese. The kind from a goat.

≈ ≈ ≈ ≈ ≈

We lie in bed, our second time, when neither of us knows ourselves.
"I'd be a salmon. And you?" I ask.

"Oh, I'm the walrus…"
I shove his shoulder: "Don't be derivative! Try again."

Refusing my game, he stretches his arms behind his head.
I sidle close, one leg thrust over; one finger loops his chest hair.

"You're a manatee…"
"No, I'm a shark."

"In your dreams," I whisper.
In actual fact, he's a manatee trapped on a desert island.

(He's a man.)

≈ ≈ ≈ ≈ ≈

If you were a fish, you'd have been a person. Small but perfect. Slits for gills and rounded lips. Your fins would ripple as you laughed. I picture you beyond the glass. You dart away, you move so fast—reverse direction, undetected—switch of time cut from the fluid. All I see is undulation, whorling where you might have been.

#5.

"Mama, where does the ocean come from?"

I'd teach you. He taught me. Not oceans, but lifetimes. We met at a conference. I flew home the next day; he gave me a lift in his rusting truck. In the holders for coffee were cores of apples: two of them, a pair of hunger. Perched and sitting side by side… I strapped my belt; he looked in the rearview. A man at the wheel—till he fumbled his keys.

"Are you sure you have my number?" he asked.

"Mama, where does the *ocean* come from?"

We live in Berkeley: a little house, a little life. It wasn't mine. My life was yours. But you escaped, so I wrote books. You loved the marina, just like your dad. He used to run each afternoon. Now he owns dogs. "I'll swim to China!" you would've said. You'd point to the sea and kick your legs. "Whatever you want," he would've replied. And he would've meant it.

He's fierce that way. He's loyal. I killed him.

Tracy Chapman sits on a stool and sings a song. Her voice is mournful, or maybe it's me. The car is fast. He drove a truck. I climbed aboard and spotted the apples. I felt the temptation to sneak the fruit, to place its curve against my lips. There was a moment. Maybe we could've. He held my hand but didn't speak. I turned toward him; he was watching the screen. She sat on a stool. No one was crying, not even the babies. The carpet was green. The children were reading with mothers and aunts—all except one boy, who stared at us. A heavy gaze. Each time I glanced in his direction: that boy was still staring. The ceiling was low. The boy was alone. We were given a number, like at a deli.

"But how is the ocean *made*!"

I always forget the tenacity of children. Single-minded, one thick root that's hard to hack. The snags of detail not yet formed. They scraped you out. They came and went. One man, two women: chatting while I lay on the table. They say it's suction, but I felt scrape. Tenacious child. Then the sound. 'I understand,' I heard myself think. It's the *sound* that's suction—a motor, a vacuum—it's almost as if I'm cleaning the kitchen. "You make such a mess," I chuckle softly. I shake my head. I vacuum the crumbs as I talk to myself because you're not here. You're at the marina with your dad. Good thing, I think. Now I can tidy up in peace.

"But *mama*—!"

I'm sorry, sweetie. I *know* the answer. I shouldn't have waited. We met at a conference. He's such a great teacher. It's caused by collision: the comets and asteroids smashed into earth. They were rich with water. Or maybe it's caused by volcanoes.

#6.

My personal was political. My womb the size and shape of her mouth. She seethed at me as we stepped from the clinic. The words hissed crimson, froth from her lips: *"Murderer!"* Her face contorted. She thrust a poster: a photo of the mangled unborn. "Let's go," he said; I couldn't move.

I wanted to tell her that I was grieving. That it was my right, and that part of that right was the right to grieve.

"You killed your baby," she leered at me.
A gob of shame bled down my leg.

I wanted to tell her. I thought I'd explain.

#7.

My nephew was drowned as a Navy SEAL but now he's beside
me, face down in the water. I think he sees bottom. He flipped
his hair like teenagers do: he stood, abrupt, and water shot from
his head in an arc. He'll die while in service. His brain becomes
plankton and algal bloom. He wants to protect us. 'The only
protection is not to be born.' That's what *you* would've said;
you would not get along. But that doesn't matter anymore.

Snails have nestled in his hair.

In Kuwait, the oil fields were set on fire: a billion barrels up
in flames. This war was the first. It's a longer series—one step
follows—'Left right left!' right into Iraq—until my nephew
marched into place. He was only a boy when the wells were
exploded. They burned for months, formed lakes of oil six feet
deep. His skin was pale before the ash. The jaw of a soldier, but
eyelashes like a luscious girl.

We eat Doritos on the deck. My legs are dangling over the side. "It's called 'port,'" he says, adjusting the mainsail. The spray of saltwater contains a danger: I savour the fantasy. "We need to tack…" He tracks the movement of a tanker—tons of metal bearing down, a hull of crates all crammed with bananas.

They feed that mush to babies; it's safer.

The shadow falls: the tanker's crates have blocked the sun. Incredibly close, our boat starts bobbing in its wake. He pulls me back as I slide toward the edge. "Oh, Aunt Marianne…" He smiles gallantly, shaking his head. But facts are facts: it gets cold on the water when islands of dead fruit float past.

The first time I sailed in San Diego you were nearby, but I didn't know. It's a desert with water: *Fertility Clinic*. Your wife didn't cry when they told her the news.

She screamed; she couldn't stop.

They could hear her in the waiting room. In time, the nurse will escort you (discreetly) out the back door. It's upsetting to others.

The pressure of water made jewels in his lungs. We could swim in his rib cage: a cavern of rubies. An avalanche, his mother's grief. She's stoic, a Spartan. She'll walk behind the flag-draped casket. Uniformed men will fold that flag: a perfect bundle. They'll place it, gently, in her arms. Then the guns go off.

"All hands on deck!"

The larger fish will eat the smaller: this is the way. The loss is ranked: a fetus aborted, a second trimester, a boy (who's a man) who's killed in war. The tankers are lurking—they'll only give way to naval ships—but our boat is rented. I trip on the lines. I'm unsure what to grieve, what to fear. Dangle port.

#8.

We were 'young and in love,' a cliché that's true. Like liquid sunshine through the veins: 'young love' can't mean anything while you're in it, then you've left it—exiled into middle age. From here, I can *know*, but I'll never *sense*—not anymore. I'm banned and barred from ever reentering: youth, innocence, ignorance.

Time, I now know. Time is an erosion.

≈ ≈ ≈ ≈ ≈

In the interim, you had three fetuses. None was born. Each was fed by hope so rich with blood but, in the end, the marriage couldn't survive the death.

In the interim, I had two children, got married/divorced, wrote five books. I spent exceeding years alone. Life dredged me dry, but I kept flooding. Pen like depths, abyss of the ocean; inside my bed I found a carcass, gnawed its bones. When dreams got bad, my son would amble. "Climb on in…" I'd lift the blanket, give him room. We drifted, anchored, safe with each other. The smallest bodies balance the oceans: plankton, algae, tiny toddler baby boy who needs his mom in times of heave. But that was many years ago. Now he's adolescent. His dreams are wet; the voice from his mouth is an animal thing. It's a wolf. He is sheepish. He's not yet familiar.

(When you were his age, your father died. But that's a lurch of time and tides and this is supposed to be stratifying.)

≈ ≈ ≈ ≈ ≈

After the interim, you arrived at my door. You invited me in, then you slowly disrobed me. I sipped my wine; I held your gaze. Defiant, to protect my shame. It's seventeen years. It's the gap, the grief, you reach across—you're reaching to touch me—return me to an older sensation. Time exists here, all at once, but only as our aging, bodies.

Now, I briefly know.

#9.

He rarely calls me by my name. The word is the deepest place in the ocean: my *given* name, if spoken in Greek. With the stress penultimate—*Mariána*—this is the deepest. Without that accent, the sound spreads, tepid—waves which never seem to crest.

Most often, he'll call me by my last. It's long, it's clunk. He slaps it, hard: a good and solid ethnic name. *Apostolides*, spoken by his Jewish tongue. He pulls me close. But I need the first. "I need you to say it…"

He calls me 'Ms. M.' when we're feeling alluvial. Voice is balanced, hint of threat. I like its heft when in my hand. "Ms. M.," he says, but I crave the drop to the furthest water. "Please," I say. *Please say my name…*

A name is a word, which is merely an arrow. It points to a 'me' who's an outline that actions. My name takes on 'meaning' within an ocean: warm-salt wash of mutual knowing. It's only with him that I feel this reaction; I want to explore it, linguistically.

≈ ≈ ≈ ≈ ≈

The actual place—the trench Mariana, within the Pacific—was recently given a nickname, too. It's *Challenger Deep*, the lowest point on planet earth. A handful of men have braved the descent: they thrilled to conquer 'Mariana,' a darkness seductive because of its depth. These men wanted monsters, or possibly fish of superfluous beauty. But things went wrong: the window cracked, the fluid leaked, the starboard thrusters lost their power. The Swiss oceanographer spotted a flounder; the lone Canadian saw a shrimp. (Though the flounder was probably only a cucumber.)

≈ ≈ ≈ ≈ ≈

At the very beginning of our expedition, I dipped my toes to test the heat: I sent an email, an open command. "Tell me one word," I wrote.

"Marianne," you replied.

#10.

Seagrass spreads in the Mediterranean, beds of fronds and roots like ginger. No other flower survives in saltwater. Despite this uniqueness, seagrass migrated from the ocean: half a billion years ago, it abandoned the sea and sprang on dry land. By adjusting its life to arid air, it bore small fruit—but then it reversed—an arduous journey, transitioning back after millions of years. It's been seventeen. You lay me down. I sense, immediate: you are my home. You're both lover and family. Return to the water. A meadow of seagrass has started to flower.

≈ ≈ ≈ ≈ ≈

The peaks of heat don't coincide: the air warms faster than the ocean. Even if we wilful, change, the oceans will retain what we've done.

The lapse will last the life of a child.
It's happening, slowly: the heat is rising on its arc.

≈ ≈ ≈ ≈ ≈

I'm on that curve. Your palms press down, atop my hips. I'd long forgotten; now I remember, this hungering touch from the time before. When we were young. When 'time' was an arrow: trajectory, forward, we'd straddle that arrow of time and ride. "And maybe that's the end of youth…" "Stay *here*," you say. You put on a record: Coltrane's ache that's coated in smoothness. My body obeys, but my mind is spinning. Restless, thinking, *this* is when we're tossed from youth: when we know, with our instinct— our animal bodies—that time is not an ever-forward. *Stay here*, you said. Your fingertips are stroking my skin. But time curves, with gravity, back.

≈ ≈ ≈ ≈ ≈

The mass of time is being released. Feedback loops as fossils burn—as seas are rising, moisture gathering.

Human minds deny this loop.

Ingenious, technology—we'll devise incredible solutions!
Rocket time: invent a future; escape the past.

≈ ≈ ≈ ≈ ≈

Waves of time are waves of sound: it's a thought experiment. Let's play it out. We're lying in bed, with an old recording of Cannonball Adderley setting the mood. "Mercy, Mercy, Mercy," he says, then he lifts his sax. In my analogy, waves of time could come together: intersect and cause a spike. An augmentation, rising toward a plane of perception that I couldn't reach without you. But you cried this morning, recalling a miscarriage. Twins, you told me. I hadn't known. I'd never seen you cry before. Continue the thought. In my analogy, waves of time could cancel each other. Arcs, in contact, suddenly flatline: an ugly, immediate, nullification. As if each history never happened. "Babe?" I say. You don't respond. You're lost in the music. Nice and flow: *Mercy, Mercy, Mercy.*

#11.

There's no illumination here. We need to imagine, this place in our mind. Our origin, inside the ocean—a passage called 'hydrothermal vents.' I'll parse that scientific language, find the fissure… Plumes of smoke, their blackness cut by flares of magma; towers thick and volatile, laden with minerals from the core. Extremes of polarity: tumult due to wild contact— geysers, jetting, searing water—surging into frigid seas. Within this intensity, microbes make sugars from chemical energy.

That's how life on earth began.

≈ ≈ ≈ ≈ ≈

We flutter in the rage of time.
We stand at the breach, as the leap, of becoming.

This liminal 'nowhere' where life must start.
But attraction gathers into a boundary: a body.

"I need to talk about the abortion…"
You pull back, abrupt: "I've moved on," you say.

≈ ≈ ≈ ≈ ≈

We don't speak for a while. Alone with your silence, I write my book. As part of the research, I listen to audio from the ocean: whales, dolphins, then the hydrothermal vents. At first, I hear nothing. This empty space—then pulse precipitates— listening, closer, my breath in suspension. Eluding me, but I remain. Attuning, or asking… I've sensed this before, with the midwife beside me, her hand on my belly: the stethoscope, the possibility. I heard it, distinctly: *it could be*, for us. We could be, a beginning—

But it's only an energy. I can't seem to make it something real.

#12.

If we heated one cubic foot of the ocean, we'd have two pounds of pure salt. I hold that white rock in my hands. My past was contained in a sturdy box. It was one foot by one foot by one foot in volume. She had ten toes. You sent me an email. I didn't expect it: the weight of our history in my mouth. Two pounds of salt. You asked me whether we might have a future. I want to say "yes," but the word won't come. All that's poured, when I speak, is the deadness.

≈ ≈ ≈ ≈ ≈

What is the language to talk of abortion? The language of 'rights' is too limited: its logic and lawfulness place it firmly within the mundane. The mysterious crux of abortion, therefore, is denied. But the language of 'ethics' is slippery, sliding—so easily—inside the throat of religion. Unable to find the proper words, my only recourse is this plea: the prayer that someone will offer forgiveness.

Not you—that's too forcibly therapeutic.

Not 'her,' as a fetus—that's too New Age.

But nor can I forgive myself—despite what yoga instructors say.

Once, we sought solace within the hands of ordained religion. (My body recalls the safety of sandalwood—incense and chanting—the voice of the priest as loving authority.) But life as a liberal and 'liberated' woman no longer admits of this kind of power: a man endowed with the right to forgive. So I open my 'good book.' My pilgrimage starts with the letter A.

≈ ≈ ≈ ≈ ≈

The 'amnion' comes from an object, in Greek; it's the bowl which holds the victim's blood. It was used in the sacrifice, primal religions when 'god' wasn't some transcendent perfection. They followed the ritual: slaughter the animal, catch its blood within the bowl. Be purged of your past as you pour that warmth inside your mouth.

"Should we schedule a visit?" you ask in an email.
"I'm trying to finish a draft of the manuscript. But definitely soon!"

In the margins near 'amnion,' I notice a detailed technical drawing: the fossil of an 'ammonite'—'the chambered shell of any of various extinct mollusks.' Spiky, coiling, starting in a tongue-like protrusion that leads through its interior walls. From the Latin root: 'the horn of Amen.'

Also on that page of the dictionary: 'amorous,' 'amoral' and 'amok.'
On the page with forgiveness: 'forfeit,' 'fork' and 'fornicate.'

≈ ≈ ≈ ≈ ≈

My daughter approaches. It's 10pm. I'm lying in bed, sipping herbal tea; I'm looking up the word 'remorse.' It comes from the Latin—the verb 'to bite'—but then transforms to the action 'to torment.' This constant biting causes anguish, which the word will then embody. All this leads to 'bitter regret.' But, in times long past, 'remorse' could also mean 'compassion.'

"What's up?" I ask.
"I can't figure out my math homework."

"When's it due?"
"Tomorrow," she says. She chews on her pen.

We sit together, work it out. I don't have the answer, but I ask her questions, which lead to solutions. She chomps and writes and gets it done. I tell her I'm proud. "But you've got to stop chewing the plastic!" I say. "It's almost as bad as when you were a baby!" My daughter responds by rolling her eyes. I tell her I love her and wish her goodnight. But she stops at the door.

"Oh, by the way…"
Then she tells me about her first kiss.

≈ ≈ ≈ ≈ ≈

Still seeking forgiveness, I find the word 'amnesty'—'a pardon for offenses committed.' It shares its stem with the word 'amnesia.' *Forgiveness*, it seems, requires *forgetting*. But when we remove the prefix 'a'—denoting 'lack'—a-mnesia reveals the goddess 'Mnemosyne,' Mother of Muses, whose name arises from 'mindful' and 'memory.'

This knowledge is a balm for my soul! Rejecting both amnesty and amnesia, I'll find forgiveness in acts of devotion. The goddess, Mnemosyne: writing, remembering, saving myself from this pillar of grief. I express my thoughts in a wordy email, wanting confirmation from you. The next day, you respond with a text.

"You free to talk?"

"I'm hanging with my son. He's feeling low… Middle school stuff."

"I can only imagine," you reply.

Your innocent sentence guts my theory—my declaration that writing a book could offer redemption. You didn't intend it; the meaning I read in your words is my own. My emotion unwittingly bloated your language: *I can only imagine...* a child, our child. You're never a dad. 'Writing,' I realize, might be a salve, but it's not salvation.

If you could just kiss me, I'd leave this logic. The ocean is rushing outside my door. I could let its life dissolve my guilt. Instead, I amass this desiccating thought. My words are drying into crystals: intricate, angular, perfect frustration. In a sudden, honest, burst of rage, I shove the paper off my desk. I watch it scatter—

My two-pound pile of inert words.

#13.

The ocean releases its breath like a gift. We get eighty percent of our air from the sea. I'm floating on water. My body's the space where the molecules kiss. I am lightness, oxygen. Phytoplankton, little plant: it's inspiration, exhalation. If I struggle, I will sink. Wet hand on my mouth, on my nose, I can't breathe. I get caught in my head, in the thoughts like a web. Like the fish who get caught in the nets left behind. I can feel it beneath me: an eerie deadness. Skirt around asphyxiation—column of water that's void of life. I sense its edge like a curving lip, an aggressor who nuzzles before he shows teeth. I must try to keep my mouth above water. Remain on my back, with the air, with the plankton. But plankton are causing deoxification. They're growing too thick: the same life that gives breath can then take it away. This is all out of balance. Too much too soon—

"It's over," I said.

You sat back: "That's provocative."

"No," I replied. "It's definitive."

I protect my routine: I will write each day.
It's my life, it's my breath.

"Breathe deeper," you said. Then you walked away.

A whale can dive for ninety minutes.
A squid only squirts its ink when scared.

The second trimester is weeks 14–26. During the second trimester your baby will do a lot of growing and developing. This article will explain those changes.

#14.

My blood contains one drop of molten, gold from when the earth was formed. It matches yours. Electrical touch through thousands of miles and millions of years. I could lick that gold-drop in your blood; I could suckle to draw it from its source. You know I can. This is why you fear me... *'Your hand,'* I said.

"Your hand is dead."

We were introduced after days of flirtation. Our friend had noticed: iridescent sparks between us. Inviting us both to a private party, he told me your name. You extended your hand—a formal gesture, deeply un-intimate—until I said my ridiculous statement. "Nice line, Marianne!" our host exclaimed; a pixie smile played on his lips.

"Am I...?" I asked, my voice sincere: "Am I inaccurate?"

Your muscle pulsed. I *knew* your hand was drained of blood: withholding your energy, you weren't ready. Even so, I shouldn't have spoken. You pulled away. The guests arrived. That could've been the end of it. But sunset, as night fell, became a brazen glow on the porch. I found our host: "I don't think I was," I whispered to him. He winked at me—then placed a capsule in your palm.

The conference is over, but waves keep pouring: lap the ecstasy into the body... Perception skews: light bends as it enters. An activist joins me; I listen to his urgent intelligence. Darkness, ardent, then he laughs at something you've said—a scattering, dazzling sound in the twilight—the sunshine that scintillates under the waves. I gaze at the man. Lustrous hair and ebony eyes; odd angle of bone or proportion of limb. I don't ask any questions. He smiles at me. His disease is autoimmune, he says. "I'm sorry..." I answer. "Why?" he asks.

The woman beside him is silent, shy. She's also (undeniably) drop-dead gorgeous. He rubs her neck, then eases his fingers down her back. Her lips are full; I don't think she's spoken a word that night. She's scared of her beauty: I see it clearly. I want to engage her in conversation, but sound is physical. (Words are softer at her edges.) Human perception can't cope with the speed: the sound waves travel faster in water. "We met at a rally," she says to me. He holds her close; she whispers to him. The sound curves over my skin.

The mermaid is chatting. I listen while massaging your forearm; I start to feel the blood drain in. "I used to be a pitcher," you say, "in the Minor Leagues." But you don't want to prove—to play this game—so you retreat. The mermaid glides closer. Electrical fields are created through motion. She plays with my hair. "I like the shirt you wore last night..." The sound is sinuous, changing speed due to temperature, pressure. It's arching now; she stretches her limbs. "I think I'm getting tired..." she says. You're watching us.

We've plunged inside the Midnight Zone. The only light is emanation: flashes of internal glow. Our host shines his gaze in my direction. He's serious mischief. Aware of the evening's tidal flows—the complex dynamics among his guests—he asks me a question. "Your first book," he says. "Have you told them about it?" The mermaid is standing—impatient, uninterested— interested only in private oceans. Salt and scent, her delicate fingers take my hand, but you engage me. Blue intensity: all other colours disappear.

This night will end with creatures in their various beds.

My hands are clasped inside of yours.

At the entry of sleeping, you confess: "You weren't inaccurate. That's why…" But your voice slips off, becomes a breath. You're trustful, already, inside this embrace.

That's why, you fear me.

#15.

Maybe we shouldn't have been so gleeful, but we couldn't help it: we ate avocados that afternoon. We hopped the fence and stole from a tree. Illicit, trespass: we hid in the sunlight. The grass was broad against my back. Such abundance in orchards. When I'd had my fill, you took me to main street—where flip-flops and surfboards—we stepped through the door and the light got dim. This store was cramped, the size of secrets; dust of dried things, smell of dandruff; all walls lined with wooden shelves. They were crammed with jars: with bark and leaves, or mushrooms and spices, the hairy balls of nuts or something. You pointed them out. Your fingers smelled like fruit and sex. He sneered at our laughter; he wore tinted glasses, a hippy who'd shed his sense of humour. "How can I help you?" he dryly asked. We explained our problem.

I didn't take hormones; you didn't like condoms.
We rhythmed on method, but wanted a further boost of sterility.

"A common request."

I would drink the tea with religious conviction.
It's all peach and swell, like the surfers in sunny Santa Barbara.

Several months later, we called from Berkeley. He told us the dosage for Penny Royal. Scoop and mix and hot and steep. "No charge for the advice." We thanked him profusely.

"But if it doesn't work…" he warned.

We didn't consider the end of that sentence. We knew it would work. Like we know that the sun. Like we know that we wake: *this will work*. It has to.

"But if it doesn't…"

I drank the brew. A spot of tea, a spot of blood. That's how it should've: quite benign. She would've been a heavy flow, an extra pad, another couple days' annoyance. Not a child. It's the abortion—the *surgical* abortion—that made her a child.

"It's love," you said.

We sat on the bed and ate popcorn and waited. "When people are in love, their bodies rev up to make babies…" Your statement served to reassure me: maybe we didn't do anything wrong. Who are *we* to thwart this force of creation?

I ate the popcorn from your hand.

That's the moment—of all the moments from our past. That one, for me, holds the heaviest sadness. It forms a sac, a membrane that carries the liquid weight of years of pain.

The irony of it…
Despite a terribly, unhappy marriage: I have two children.
You have none.

Every visit to the bathroom: trepidation, expectation… Your wife's blood was fresh and vivid; I scraped my inner in hopes of red. For both of us, you paced outside the door.

Squids will grip their mates in the ocean, their tentacles turning a brilliant red. Glowworms emanate creamy light, like the cool of the moon in erotic coyness. Sea stars raise their arms and arch; they spray their crimson sex on their chosen. Corals spawn one day a year. The whole sea frenzies: scent of readiness, coral estrus, after the summer's brightest moon.

You credited 'love.' I wish I could be so romantic about it.

The shop in Santa Barbara has changed—at least in my imagination. The oil spills have brought the tide: the pipes have burst, the rig mistakes, the shorelines smeared. The jars are filled with relics of oceans:

- the ulcerated stomachs of sea lions;
- gills of a stingray, sealed with tar;
- the lesioned eyes of an octopus;
- a dolphin's lung which hemorrhaged blood
  (its blowhole had got plugged with crude).

The oil was spilling back then, too—but I didn't notice at the time: I wasn't yet sullied enough to see it.

#16.

The decision was mutual. How do we define 'mutual'?

We take it for granted: we flush, and it all gets taken away. There's a party at our house, with laughter and music. I sit on the toilet. Around the world, the number of people who lack sanitation is 2.6 billion. It's very awkward: a weird little dance to catch pee on a stick. I need spatial reasoning. *Two lines equal...*

≈ ≈ ≈ ≈ ≈

They say the test takes a full three minutes. Tick the clock: each second counts. In developing nations, they dump almost ninety percent of the sewage. It's raw and untreated. It's teeming with typhoid and hepatitis. Lungs are spongy. Stare at the stick: nothing's happening yet; maybe nothing will! The music stops, a pause between songs. In the gap comes the garble of conversation. Senses are heightened at times of stress. The bathroom is clean. We're having a party. We're laughing, but children are constantly dying—they die from the sewage—they say 1.4 million every year...

This year I'm turning twenty-four. Today is my birthday. The party is mine. You've bought me a dress, which I'm sweating through. My pits are wet. The first line bolds. This serves for comparison—nothing more. It doesn't mean anything—not on its own. Alone in the bathroom, I catch a glimpse: the line is pink. What a *hideous* colour to choose for this test! Like baby-girl sweetness with cute little ribbons. But water in harbours is turning brown: it's churning the fecal. The waste from cows is termed the 'effluent.' Really, it's shit. The cows' manure is causing the dead zones: the strangulation of expanse of water. My chest is tightness; I feel nauseous. Sewage is bypassing treatment plants. It overflows in heavy downpours. Even a five-minute burst of rain…

It's been two minutes. I look at my watch. The stick is steeping in my pee. The line is faint: a haunting or mocking. I pace in the bathroom—a half-step forward, then I pivot. Spinning in circles. I glance at the stick each time I turn. The watch's hand relentlessly rotates. With each passing second, the colour gets darker. It's scarlet and shameful: the slashes of heat start to brighten my cheeks. With a shivering panic, I leave the bathroom, grab your hand. Apologizing to the guests, you follow me. I lock the door. You don't understand why I'm acting this way. I'm the only one who saw the lines…

Besides, I feel it in my nipples.

'Mutual' is a Latin word: 'received and directed in equal amounts.'
The decision was mine.

If I'd said I wanted to keep the baby, you would've knelt to
the floor in an instant. With my hand in yours, you would've
proposed: a life, a marriage, a mutual effort to grow and love.
I know this is true. The choice of whether to abort must reside
in the woman, since this is where the embryos lodge.

The decision was mine, though the baby was ours.
It's a quandary I haven't been able to rest.

We pass through stages. First is denial. Like zooming forward: leave it behind at the speed of suction. Then comes the punishment: self-flagellation, the guilt unabated. Infliction of pain is the only solution. And then, if you're lucky, you'll get mature. But that's not guaranteed—especially not with the 'hormone pollution' and useless distraction.

Just look at the intersex on the screen.

Those 'intersex' fish are hybrid and impotent: sexual organs have been malformed. Our birth control pills have made them sterile; sometimes 'males' make eggs in their testicles. Due to synthetic hormones in urine, fish take estrogen through their gills. But *I'm* not 'polluting.' I'll only discard one embryo, and the pills I take will be for the cramping.

This space requires humility—this room where we're stripped of human pretension, the body laid bare.

We showered together, the morning after we'd first shared a bed. We were shy with each other, the lights too bright in the hotel bathroom. We shut them off and showered in darkness. The water was streaming; I tilted my head, felt your mouth on my neck. Take your fist to the sink in the hospital bathroom: you told me the story. You slammed to the bone. Miscarriage of justice: miscarriage of fetus, but cancer was spreading inside your mom. You cared for her through months of illness, carried her gently from bathroom to bed. I would place my children in the tub. Divorced, our lives were split down the centre. My knees on the tiles, my kids cried like murder when I washed their hair. But I bathed you the first time I saw you, after. Seventeen years. With steam on our nakedness, I sponged the years like grime off your skin—drew the towel, slow, across your chest—your lips, your eyes, you let me cleanse. When I was done, you lifted your hand to touch my cheek. The droplets fell from your skin to the water.

You spoke soft words and sought my gaze. But I focused elsewhere, watching the ripples. "Don't thank me," I finally answered.

#17.

He'd held my hand in the waiting room. Her fingers are forming. She now has ten: 'ten fingers and toes,' that's what everyone says. I lie uncomfortably on the bed, my skin exposed. The ultrasound tech tells me to relax. The gel is cold on my belly.

"Can my partner be in here?"
"No," says the tech. "Partners can't be in treatment rooms."

"Why?" I ask.
"*Why…?*" she replies. That's all she says.

"Why?" I insist.
"Because we don't want men coercing women to have abortions."

Incredulously, I ask my question: "Does that really happen?"
"Yeah," she sighs. "That really happens."

In the darkened room, the light from the screen reflects off her face. I look at the contours, shadowed and grey. I decide not to vocalize what I'm thinking: that in the densely crowded waiting room, I could count the number of men on one hand.

The tech is staring at the screen; her wrist is rotating, expertly seeking, without ever looking at my body. She presses the wand on my wall of muscle. She's probing for vital information: the exact location of tissue to excise.

"Wait," I say when the tech is done.
"Wait...?"

"I want to see it..."
"You want to *what*?"

"I don't know *why*, but—"
"Listen," she responds: a steady tone. "Do you want this abortion?"

"I want this abortion."
But I want to see it.

Silent questions pass between us. Static, uncertain, she finally swivels the screen toward me. The hollow picture—shadows of echoes—projects an image of my centre. I shrink back from the portrait I see: a helpless child, terrified, as I lie on the bed.

#18.

They hovered in white gowns and white sheets, a wonderland of ghostly fluorescence. Suspended from movement and animation... I'm gliding in, a succulent weakness, to take my place among the listless. "Are they okay?" I ask the nurse. He nods: "They're recovering."

Unlike the others (dozens of others) I've asked for local anaesthesia.

The fish disengage from their surroundings. It's hard to arouse them; it's not like the 'normal' sleep of mammals. Trance-like phase of non-response. The mind is restful, free from sensory— sealed off as the world streams past. Tranquility that's born of absence. Silently, I slide among them.

Floating, dreamlike…

Fish will sleep amidst vegetation—inside of a sponge, or buried in sand. For us, it's rows of medical beds. I'm placed in the third row. The women around me don't seem to notice: they're lacking engagement with the outside world. They're not 'awake,' but we can't call it 'sleep.' It's the amniotic bliss of amnesia.

The anaesthesia wears off slowly.

The girl beside me has hundreds of freckles; they're windswept across her prairie cheeks. Her hair is brown. I don't know the colour of her eyes: her lids are drooping. Amongst all fish, it's only sharks whose eyes have lids. But sharks can't sleep! Nature's humour is quite sadistic; sometimes laughter comes from fear.

During sleep, we consolidate sensory: gather experience into a body.

Sleep is not the same as unconsciousness.

Anaesthesia binds the neurons.

Myriad proteins, on dendrites and ethics, will no longer function.

The women were floating like virginal angels, lobotomized beauties.

The memory of the 'event' is missing.

What's my 'life,' if not an event?

"Please," I said. Please tell me what's happening.

"This one's awake," the doctor said. Such surprise in his voice. They can say shit like that when the women are sleeping: unconscious maidens, blank for proceeding. "Please tell me what's happening…" One man, two women. Another man enters. I think he's a nurse. Now I'm cleaning the crumbs off the floor at home. The carpet is green. You're trapped in the waiting. I never asked you what you were thinking. "What's *happening*?!" The vacuum is scary. The sound frightens children. It's over in seconds. They look at the body-part: flesh and nozzle, node of tissue. The nurse, though: he has looked in my eyes. "They're about to remove the embryo…" Kindness, to tell me. To treat me humanely. It's *she* who's not human: she's only a fetus. But I'm a woman; it's my right.

"Please," I panted.

Maybe the man was an orderly; they didn't say why he was there. He might've carried bleach for the table. The hordes of women were waiting their turn. They were holding their number. The doctor only held a hose. And it kept getting longer: a white-worm sea creature in the depth. "They've removed the embryo…" Clean the equipment. We must fully sterilize. Someone else will be here soon. The hallways seemed like glaring tunnels—stark light, doors—that took me toward the cavern of women. The nurse must've wheeled me, unless he's an orderly. Clearly, I can't recall his face. My vision was voided. The features were suctioned, removed by the vacuum. Please tell me: I can't remember his eyes. But he spoke to me. He treated me like I was a person.

They handed me a bundle of clothes and a box of juice which contained a straw. I spoke with the girl who has numerous freckles. We drank our juice. I don't remember the many transitions. I lay on a bed amidst resting coral, then I'm holding my jeans and my socks. My juice was apple mixed with sugar. They asked me to drink before getting dressed. The girl is young, then I'm in the change room. It's not a 'room,' just curtains draped from metal rods. I zip my jeans. The woman beside me has dropped her panties on the floor; I'm watching her fingers pick them up. My eyesight is shaky. Or maybe the shaking is her hand.

The 'sixth extinction' is coming fast. I can't comprehend it: I can't put a scene to this phrase that will happen. *A mass extinction*—a magnitude of devastation, exceeding my imagination. Still, I want to be awake. Whatever happens, I *will* be awake. The slumberous maidens taught me that. A vision so supremely repulsive: the stupor amidst the mistakes we made.

≈ ≈ ≈ ≈ ≈

The girl with the freckles has large brown eyes.

They're deep like woods, like trees cut down.

This was her third abortion, she said.

#19.

Tectonic plates glide over skeletal remains. Our foundation of crust lies on pulverized bone. It's white, like the talcum used for babies. *Please don't cry.* There are trillions of dead; they're microbial things. It's scientific: I've got proof. But you're the one with the PhD. I only write stories. They'd fit in the unhinged jaw of an eel.

We don't discuss it. "There's nothing to say!" I want to believe we can carry forward, as we'd been, but tectonic plates grind beneath our feet. Like the groan when Gaia gave birth to the skull. Then Pangaea was cleft; it ached like the bone of my calcium pelvis. Pry apart what once cohered. There was an 'us' which drifted.

≈ ≈ ≈ ≈ ≈

After the abortion, you suggest a submersible. Send probes down, wear protective gear. The therapist takes the cheque at the end. She tells us her couch is an 'island of safety.' I don't like her metaphors, or her lipstick. Her couch is a rowboat that's tossed in the ocean. The water heaves; I quell the squall. I focus on small: there are worms in the ocean. Identify, classify, thousands of species. They're sleek or segmented, with frills near their mouths. They grow bulbous or smooth; they can stretch thirty metres. The therapist pinches. I answer succinctly, but it won't stop. She pulls the worm and it keeps coming:

body, throbbing, from my throat. She's unperturbed. I wonder whether she knows what she's doing. (She knows too well.) Proboscis extends. But after the second session, I quit.

"I can't do it," I say. "I don't have the language…"

That's bullshit, I realize: what I lacked was *depth*.

'Language' is easy. It's human that's hard.

≈ ≈ ≈ ≈ ≈

The ocean's currents gyre and vortex around the globe. One current took us north, to Alaska, but then the ocean overturned: a vertical plunge as the dense water heavies. This happens when ice begins to form. We could've expected, but I wasn't ready. We drifted on skeletons. Blue lips stiff and muscle bone. Why think of this? Why talk and tentacle? Words and 'process' can't stop precipitous. I only wanted to fun and fuck: I was young and in love, but the shame is unspeakable. You only wanted to drive to Alaska: to use the oil, pump the fossil, buy electrical goods from abroad. I don't *want* a 'safe island' for 'processing feelings,' not when the tankers lurk toward shore. Who am *I* to determine what lives in the ocean? Regardless of me, when this process ends—regardless of *us*—the fish will slipper through sapphire water… Leave them be.

"Please leave me *alone!*"

Please, give me time: I'll find the depth.

I'll sink to the place where language forms.

#20.

If he was there, I don't recall. The railing was there. My hip
bones were there. They were pressed against the bar of metal.
Torso forward: I looked down. Our ship was slicing through the
sea—this pristine coolness, wilderness off the coast of Alaska.
Alcohol was served down below.

≈ ≈ ≈ ≈ ≈

A pod of dolphins skimmed along, beside the ship: a constant
rotation, propulsion in dynamic waves. "They're playing with
us!" I heard him exclaim. But their motion seemed driven, devoid
of joy. My voice was defensive: "That's my opinion, okay?"

They say the glacier groans as it calves; they say the resulting
icebergs shudder. I don't remember what I said to set him off.
The ship cut its engines and silence ensued. I hadn't realized
how angry, that engine, had clogged my ears. Adrift within the
alien landscape: blocks of ice were gliding, aimless, colourless
in the scattered light. The sun was weak on the upper deck.
Immense emptiness: people were elbowing for a view.

The melting of glaciers is causing the level of oceans to rise.
Islands are vanishing.

'Dis-appearance'—as a concept—is elusive.

We'll often concoct an array of stories.
But 'gone-ness' is hard for the mind to conceive.

I longed for the dolphins, for movement to give me a focal point. Instead, I faced the frozen edifice. The crevasse was yawning down the sheer; the ice glared blue from dense compression. Watching, waiting, for pieces to fall. "Isn't this great?" I didn't respond. A seabird's cry was ricocheting off the chill. Evaporation swathed my skin: a fine mist, I breathed it in, and started to shiver. Tremendous quaking: "I'm not cold," I said, when he tried to touch me.

What I recall is the slow-motion nature. The chunk of ice pulled away from the glacier. Excruciating, anticipation—the bead of tension—rising in the lapse of time. We *know* what will happen: this glacial yield. Yet we'll stare, transfixed, as it does.

≈ ≈ ≈ ≈ ≈

I think you spoke when the ice came down—
But the brute force drowned you, out.

#21.

Maybe he lived in a mangrove forest. He's taller than redwoods. His limbs are ancient. Trunk of trees, I'll shimmy their bark. I'm alone at the festival. Layered waves of booming sound. The musicians are men, but the dancers are women: ibex torsos, onyx and glisten. They wear a dress of cowrie shells. Exuberant, music: I follow their movement, but I can't do it—awkward and effort and gawk-imitation. I close my eyes. I'd smoked alone, which I never do. But you were busy. You were working. This festival didn't interest you.

It interested me.

Salinity will kill the trees. Five drummers on stage, with their slaps overlapping. Rewetting the drumhead, an intersection of land and sea. A mangrove forest: adaptive, responsive, with aerial roots. I lift my arms. The music will lead me. My body has never moved like that. My blood is Greek; it channels the flow of my muscle and limbs. But the roots will breathe. They're dense and tangled, interlocking. One quick stroke, and I'm sinuous rolling. The Greek sense of longing, a dissonant ache in minor key: this is my body. His drums taught me different. This man, this musician from Senegal.

Late that night, I shook his hand. His palms were cakes of dried mud: each lifeline a fissure. A slab of earth that's cracked from drought. His drum was slung. A goat's hide stretched. The man knows rhythms, when to pause. *"Vous* **êtes** *belle,"* he said, *"quand vous dansez..."* *"Comment?"* I replied. He laughed; I blushed.

"Etes-vous canadienne?"
"Américaine... Et vous?"
"Je suis sénégalais. J'ai habité au forêt de—"

He used to live in a mangrove forest, until his home got choked by roads. He lives, instead, on the festival circuit. He seemed nostalgic: the mangroves made honey and sheltered the fishes; they stopped the erosion of soil and culture. But progress is forward, and thieves come at night.

"Je ne comprends pas..."
He's speaking to me; I don't understand.
(I'm American, so I barely speak French.)

"The number of Africans threatened by floods will be 70 million..." The West must cut its greenhouse emissions by forty percent, or people will die. "The drought will intensify in the interior." Grain won't grow: a loss of fifty percent of yield. Both flood and drought, depending on where...

This is not what he says.
I don't know what he says.
"Mais, j'aime beaucoup votre rhythmes."

He led me to a quiet corner, hoping I could catch his meaning.

"*Aimez-vous danser?*" he asked.

"Yes." Yes, I like it…

Eat the bark of a mangrove tree. A splinter sucked, the reed of a sax. I knew I would leave you. There was no betrayal. No touch except the shake of hands. No lust except the vision of cowrie. This wasn't seduction of bodies felled on a waiting bed. This seduction was darker: a darkness most radiant.

"*Etes-vous danseuse?*"

"*Non,*" I said. "*Je suis écrivaine…*"

And with that, the balance of oceans shifted.

#22.

The glorious union of death and fuck was never so obvious as in a salmon. Freud's cigar would be ashamed. It's eros-pulse in silver scales. The meat is pink and tender.

≈ ≈ ≈ ≈ ≈

We went to see the salmon run. (The 'he' in 'we' refers to another: the man I'd marry. The man I'd spawn.) "You gotta see it." Leap past rapids, sex and compulsion. I brought my journal. I wanted 'experience.' Reference my 'I': I would be a writer. It was exciting; he'd purchased a camera for making movies. His syntax was consciously avant-garde.

He swung the lens toward a teen in the water whose arms were plunged—his ass raised high—just like the Greek. I felt an uncomfortable rush of remembrance: the warmth before the rub and come. I wrote it down. The body thrashed, but this boy was harmless: swagger stance and pimples puss. "I got one!" he shouted. He lifted the salmon above his head. The camera zoomed. He held his trophy for our pleasure. "What's your name?" asked my future ex-husband. The boy replied, with darting gaze and fast bravado. "How'd you learn to catch fish with your hands?"

My avant-garde lover kept asking questions; he needed material. Far too long, his questions spewed. His goateed mouth was near the mic: voice loud and guffaw as compared with the teen. The subject, the starfish, but he was prey: a teenaged boy, the camera trained. Perform for us. Perform for the eye.

≈ ≈ ≈ ≈ ≈

It was sudden, revolting. Cascading from her sacs were the eggs. They spattered the pant-legs of the boy. Blood drained from his cheeks with the speed of the torrent. He understood. He looked at me, ignoring the camera. He came of age at that instant, I saw it: the dead-mother-fish in his hands. "She'll be fine," he said. He panicked and turned. He held her under, slid her gently side to side. "She just needs oxygen." Others muscled toward their end. She was dead already—though she was still breathing. She'd failed in her purpose: she'd spilled her eggs like vomit, orange, onto the dirt.

The lens switched off. I continued watching. "It's getting dark…" He'd gotten bored. I stayed where I was; I was watching the boy. He was holding her, swaying her through the water. He spoke to her softly; I couldn't hear, but saw his lips whisper. Then came the gaudy voice of the other: "You gotta see this!" He called me over. I had to see: a plastic doll in a garbage bin. Demented face, the clothes ripped off. One eye was closed; the other stared at the camera, unblinking. A smear of dirt was on her belly. "What a great shot! Look at this!"

≈ ≈ ≈ ≈ ≈

She died so close to her arrival. Miles, compulsion, she died out of water, surrounded by air she could not breathe. She must've sensed her nearness to home: to her birth and her bearing, total surrender. She must've smelled our acrid regret: the squirt of armpits, yellow awareness. I wanted to grace him, to hold him, maternal. Instead, the other called me over. *Look! A dead baby in a bin!* He was delighted. It was art.

#23.

Saturday night and the internet calls. I can't resist: I start trawling the depths, using modern equipment to increase yield. But most of the catch is too puny to keep. Then I seek your name. It's fifteen years. The hope in my chest is the size of my screen. I'm not yet old but not still young: I'm an involuntarily celibate single, a forty-something mother of two.

It's a Saturday night. Did I mention that?

≈ ≈ ≈ ≈ ≈

There are very few people who have your name.

By happy coincidence, you're one of them!

Sadly, you haven't yet joined Facebook.

≈ ≈ ≈ ≈ ≈

Fish stocks collapsing: the number of fish is declining fast. Industrial fishermen harvest the species they once rejected. It's called 'fishing down.' This is common for women in middle age. The sought-after species are already taken. Tuna, cod, intelligence, kindness: their numbers reduced by ninety percent. It's a serious problem. Especially since the fish who remain prefer girls in their twenties. (But that's an aside.)

We'll seek down the chain. We're hoping, still, for a viable catch.

≈ ≈ ≈ ≈ ≈

I could pimp myself on various websites. Instead, I add the word 'professor.' Instantaneous: your name appears. The website for searching has taken the bait… *Now* what do I do? I can 'Rate My Professor'—assess your methods, rank your toolkit—I'll evaluate your technique.

'This prof *really* gets me excited!'

The data dangle on the end of my hook. I could read the reviews; I could harvest the info like seabass and sole. I might even learn—from a sub-clause buried deep in a bio—about a child. Maybe a wife and a dog and a home. My cursor is hovering over the lure: the familiar words, your name still bolded.

"Okay," I say to my empty apartment. "This feels really creepy."

Like scurrying sideward, a crab on a beach. Like the click of my claws on the plastic keys. You always preferred the direct approach: "Your hand," I said. With the quiet dignity of a mackerel, I move away from my computer. I don't need to know what's become of you. It's enough, for then, to see your name.

#24.

You sent me an email; the wave knocked me down. Without taking off my coat and hat, I dropped to my chair. My children were arguing; sound was receding. Now all the past comes rushing in.

≈ ≈ ≈ ≈ ≈

A wave has come. It knocks me down. My cheek is dragged against the sand. There's a grain in my mouth. "Next slide," you said. I wanted to write, or to 'be' as a writer—the *qua* and pretension—the words are tumbling through my mind. I can't remember why I left—what we forgot to say in Alaska. "I don't have the language." I sit in my chair and look at your name. Hold your breath. Don't breathe. The suction starts. It screams, as I screamed, both times I gave birth—a daughter, a son—I have two children, one ex-husband, lots of books. They line my wall. Disgorge the ocean: the words from those books are like grains of sand. I've shoved that sand across the page; I've tried to give it order and meaning, but now this wave is pulling me under. "*Murderer!*" That word scrapes my skin; it's rough, it flays, like the drummer's hand. I danced on the seafloor, but Tracy Chapman sits on a stool. We never discussed. It's a gap in our able: a rift that's like a glacial moan. *Je suis écrivaine.* In the space that was emptied was my voice.

≈ ≈ ≈ ≈ ≈

The wave has spit me onto the beach. It's a heave, like nausea, and just as corrosive. I tell my kids it's time for dinner. I eat with sea kelp clumped in my hair. "What's wrong?" my son asks. "I'm not sure."

≈ ≈ ≈ ≈ ≈

I've never seen the mating of sea turtles… stingrays that fly with graceful menace. A whale is birthing underwater… thousands of fish swim like one sleek body. Jellies diaphanous, tropical luminous, corals that mesmer even the mermaids. These are all unknown to me. They belong to a realm that's called by your name.

"A lot of water under the bridge...
Here's my number, if you want to talk."

In our first conversation, you tell me about the various miscarriages of your ex-wife. In the very next breath, you recall our abortion. I wonder whether the point is to wound. Despite my discomfort, I don't disconnect: I want, to talk, to return to whatever attraction we'd shared. After several weeks, you suggest a visit.

I shouldn't continue; it's simply not logical.
(Nor is desire.) I book my flight to California.

You can't find the car in the parking garage; the bouquet of flowers makes me sneeze. I'm suddenly fearful we can't span the distance. It seems rather silly, and somewhat misguided. Like grasping at seaweed or surfing a whale. As I stand in your home, you lean back in your chair—broad chest, arms crossed—and take me in.

"You look good, Apostolides," you say.
Without further thought, I plunge.

#25.

Taste comes from the core of earth. Volcanoes, as always, are to blame. The acid was raining luxuriantly: a little stamp, I take a lick. "An object doesn't *have* a taste," I say to you. A 'taste' is always interaction: tongue to object. Complex reaction of chemical nature. The acids dissolving: Medusa snakes within my vision.

≈ ≈ ≈ ≈ ≈

"You okay?" you ask.
I'm sucking my hair.

"She was cursed," I reply.
"Does that mean you're okay?"

"Medusa was cursed, so her hair turned to snakes…
"But the rest of her," I say, "is beautiful."

I kiss your lips to prove my point.
"I never realized…"

"Would you like a taste?"
"Of your hair?"

"They're snakes."
"Sure," you say. "In a second… But first: why did they curse her?"

"Medusa had sex with Poseidon."
"Since when were the Greeks against sex?!" you ask.

"They did it inside the sacred temple; virgin Athena was very upset."
"You Greeks are so obvious…"

Oh, I say. But we have our secrets.
"Lie down," you reply.

I relax on the seafloor.
My hair flows like breath in a sexual medium.

≈ ≈ ≈ ≈ ≈

Swim with sea nymphs. Bubbles hiss from thermal vents. If I lie still, those bubbles settle. One is popping on my nipple. Take it slowly on your tongue. Bite down: it hurts. Or maybe it pleasures. But wait a minute: we were discussing! Then suddenly, you're the plume of a geyser! You shrug your shoulders: "Trips are like that. Don't try to predict them."

"I'm trying to tell you the cause of taste."
"That'd be helpful," you say.

Then your logic leaps like a whale in the breach:
"Why *do* you love me?"

"It's hard to explain…"
"I guess you'll need to demonstrate."

"But we should be serious! Just for a minute."
"Don't ruin the trip, babe. It turns on a dime."

Don't resist the roll of waves when you're tripping.
If you resist, you'll fall prey to monsters.

"Don't *say* that word!" I interject. The monster lurks inside our past. It circles, needful: muscle umbilical. "Why did you say that word?" I moan. The '*nst*' is teeth, two rows like sharks. It clamps my fearful. Nothing has happened, but any second: all this time. She's drifting, lost, in the undersea amnion. Tighten my muscle: I hear the growl of the engine, the suction. Her jaws, they are opening. Hideous wailing: the accusation of unborn grief.

"Don't resist it," you say. "I'm right here."
"She's right here."

You will always be here.
You're part of my plasma.

You place your hand atop my belly.
"Just breathe into me."

≈ ≈ ≈ ≈ ≈

"Better now?" you ask. You've made the coffee.
"I've always loved you…"

"That's great," you say. "But you haven't said *why*."
Why does the ocean taste primordial?

"It's all about magma."
"You're too metaphoric!"

"I'm not!" I reply. "I'm describing geology!" Listen: it's simple.
"With *you*, nothing's simple."

I seahorse your atoll and speak like a petal: "That's why you
love me…" "Just answer the question."

It's ancient volcanoes: they made acid rain, which then leached
the salt, which ran into oceans…

You nod your head.

Then some of it seeped through the flow to the mantle, erupting
again, but now bursting with elements.

You sip your coffee.

"In other words…" When you taste the ocean on my lips, you're
tasting the mineral core of earth. "Did I get it right?"

You totally nailed it.

#26.

I saw you at your wedding. You were turning away: half a smile, a surety. I can almost map your gestures. I pick up the photo, bring it close. Your wife is the focus; she's hugging your mom. They're both utterly happy, that cosmic glow of all possibility. You're in the background: a shadow, a profile, barely seen. I'm looking, now. I'm taken aback by how much we've changed.

≈ ≈ ≈ ≈ ≈

The tides are celestial, moving the oceans up and down. The gravity tugs, and your house gets flooded: boxes filling, junk is drifting onto the sidewalk. You'd sold the house, the 'marital home.' With a surge of hope, I come to help. After all these years, the sun and moon are in alignment! It's called a 'spring tide.' But it also means that water will bulge.

I've been weeping non-stop.

You've left to sign the dotted line. It's two small words and all is done. The lawyer has prepared the papers. "Shouldn't take long." You close the door, I pack your records: Duke was the master, your hands on my keys. You'd told me secrets late last night when jazz was our ocean, but now here's The Clash. I must pack them away. I must be alphabetical. Label the box:

Important! Fragile! This Side Up!

The orbital angle of the moon will alter the rise. It's an ebb and a flow; it's a rhythmic cycle. Tides are predictable. Grief is not. I try to squelch it: cardboard boxes fall apart when they get wet. I haven't asked you to carry the boxes, although they're heavy. You don't need my weakness; you've already got enough on your mind.

Besides, you're not even here.

You're putting your name on that piece of paper; I find a note in your ex-wife's hand. Like evidence, penmanship: this is how her fingers moved. We'd had sex that morning. You left for the lawyer's. Then I packed your books and the note fell out. I try not to read it, but her loops are floral; they're pretty and circular.

My pen is tighter and meaner than hers.

You'd told me not to pack the vase, the one that's blue. She'd asked for that. "She has good taste…" I touch the curve. She's beautiful on your wedding day. You turn away, your face in profile. Wavy hair that's gunmetal grey. Now it's lighter, like silver, and you've cut it short. I remember my fingers in your hair. I pack the photos, seal the box.

I slice my hand on the teeth of the tape gun.

I move to the kitchen. I can't stop the leaking. I don't understand this spring of tears. Inside a cupboard, I find a stash of tea she drank. I take a whiff. "It's stale and old," I tell myself. I throw it away. All the cookbooks are splattered, their pages warped. She liked to make cookies; I'll never make cookies; I really hate cookies.

I'd rather use butter in other ways.

You return from the lawyer's. I try not to cry. "Let's go out to dinner," you suggest. "Let's celebrate." I nod my head. You turn away.

The energy builds: two entities moving in different directions. They lock. They grind. Tectonic plates will hold their position. The tension accumulates. Neither gives way. This is called the 'rough spot'; it isn't sustainable. Stress must release; it can cause a tsunami. It's known as a 'seismic slip-rupture event.'

I sleep on the couch. I write you a note. I can't remember what it says: it's tighter, it's meaner. I tell you I love you, but don't know how.

A tsunami can travel the speed of a jet plane. I sit by the window and strap my belt. The pilot says to prepare for takeoff. It's six in the morning. We'd said goodbye; I woke you from dreaming. You seemed confused when I said your name. I don't think you remembered it's me.

"Goodbye," I whispered. "I'm sorry…"

I'm heading eastward, on the airplane: thirty-thousand feet above. I can't sit still. My impulse is to smash the glass—to break the window, return to your door. I've been crying for hours. The woman beside me is patting my hand. She lives in Kansas; she knows about weather, and also of home.

"You guys deserve a chance," she says.

This woman has been married twice. Her second husband is sitting beside her. He's reading a book, trying not to listen. They're coming home after months in Hawaii. They'd climbed the volcanoes. Their marriage has lasted twenty years. "Just wait for the storm to pass," she advises. "You can't decide under those conditions."

I call you when I reach dry ground.

"I'm not ready for this to end," I say. You're noncommittal, inconclusive: "I'm not sure *what* I'm ready for… I love you, but I need some time." That night, I sit on my porch in Toronto. I try to feel connected to you—to submit to this force which draws us together. I gaze at the moon: pendulous, beautiful, not quite full…

But it seems too remote to have any effect on us at all.

The third and final trimester is week 27 through the end of pregnancy. By the end of the second trimester, all of your baby's organs and body parts are present and working correctly. Now everything needs to grow and mature.

#27.

I crawl in the shell of a horseshoe crab. Through his ten
eyes, I see pterodactyls. I also see epochs of earth and my
lovers. The timescales are different; the horseshoe is nice and
accommodates me. As an elder statesman of the planet—450
million years old!—he's learned to be patient with youngsters.

≈ ≈ ≈ ≈ ≈

We'll start with you, the first man I loved, so long ago:
Carboniferous Era. The climate is warmer, with bony fish.
The ocean's expanding along with my consciousness. Ferns
are filled with vascular water; we listen to music and smoke
green plants. This era accumulates powerful energy, fuelling
centuries to come.

But crabs must molt—seventeen times in a single life.

The new skin grows beneath the shell. It's folded like a supple
fan. The water seeps; the pleats get swollen, press against
interior walls. I feel crammed in our bedroom; I want to
explore. But that festival doesn't interest you; I go alone. This
begins the first molt, which is also called the 'immature.'

≈ ≈ ≈ ≈ ≈

Horseshoe crabs always spawn at night, when the tides are high and the moon is full. It seems romantic. It's mainly a question of synchronization: nine months later, I'm engaged. He's edgy, an artist. His tail is a 'telson.' I thought, perhaps, it'd serve to inspire: my pen and my fantasies. I was a writer.

I'm so naïve.

By the time we met, his core of fossil fuels had formed. An endless store of conflagration. I thought it was passion. In fact, he's Triassic: the Age of the Reptiles. (Alligators have great smiles.) I'd show you more, but I've learned my lesson: *never* trust that a dead-still reptile is actually sleeping. Let's leave it there and move on.

≈ ≈ ≈ ≈ ≈

Blood will flow through my multiple pages. In crabs, they're 'lamellae'; they make twelve 'books.' Each book is filled with sensory cells—millions of them—which contribute to great art, and fights with our lovers. These book-gills are mainly used for breathing, except the first pair: this is where the genital pores.

Which brings to mind a poet I dated…

This guy belongs to the Mesozoic: butterflies, grasshoppers, dinosaurs, bees. He's a brilliant man who cogitates moral—and acts with his cockroach. At crucial moments, he's a marsupial: first on earth. He'll hide in his pouch, a T. Rex who hops like a kangaroo. His writing, though: his writing has integrity.

≈ ≈ ≈ ≈ ≈

The Mesozoic ends with a cataclysm, leaving a crater that's never been healed. I can feel its impact most acutely on weeks when my children are with their dad. I weep every day for a million years. (It's actually 'only' ten months of weeping. I realize one night, when I'm lying in bed: 'I haven't cried today,' I thought. This realization was a shock. I started to cry…)

Climb in the carapace: seven years of swimming alone.

I'm about to dry up on the beach of my forties, but then I meet a physical trainer. He trains me, physically, at a dojo. He's eager and able. Unfortunately, his horseshoe-brain is in his heart, is in his mouth, which is in his glands: he attaches himself to another female. They flirt at the dojo. I tell them I'm happy they've found each other—while pinning her pretty limbs to the mat.

≈ ≈ ≈ ≈ ≈

Then there's you, our second time. I come to the beach and release my scent. The birds and ex-lovers can't find us here. I'll breathe through my membrane: one leaflet expands. It's a book, it is swelling. Please take my hand. It's time, if you'll trust me. The moon is new. I've dug the place; we'll *both* be transformed. I can feel the sand. It's warm on my body; it gives us moisture. Slow at first. We'll take it slow. Our pleats are expanding; the water is filling. It's faster now. We can't control. We've entered the epoch: Anthropocene, the time of man. You're here, in the sand, in the tidal flats; together, at this moment of change. Can you shed the carapace you once wore? It can't allow us, not together. Not if you love me… Ease your body. Trust my body. Trust me: we might not survive this—molting, transforming— this loss of protection and smallness and home.

But I'll take my chances. 450 million years. It's worth a shot.

#28.

Soon we'll all be hoarding the ocean; we'll store it in cars so that we can wash them. I eat an orange that's grown in the desert. It's sun-kissed, strapless, spread your legs—but only in inquiry. Little waves come rippling.

≈ ≈ ≈ ≈ ≈

I'm back on the boat after many years. We're together, apart, but the movement is circular: currents are driven by gravity, density; contour of landmass and breast are important. We're sailing through San Diego's bay. We've been here before—but the playlist is new. J Boog fats the bass. It's down on the beat and fleshy, wet. The rhythms drop, but waves are peaking; I can feel the mainsail luffing. Pull the line, a little tighter. Touch my dress: I'm trying to understand the currents.

I eat my orange; it's blood red.

The drought gets drier; I swallow the juice.

I'm wondering whether we'll have a future.

My son is walking toward the prow. He stands like a man. He's guzzling liquid; it flows down the throat or the hose or the pipe. But the slick of oil has settled at bottom. I lotion my skin.

There are millions of gallons inside the Gulf. Despite our efforts, the carpet of crude will remain on the seafloor: a clue to the future. It lies beside the asteroid's crater, the watery gravesite for dinosaurs. I find that quite pleasing: symmetrical, almost. Symbolic or narrative, like there's a God.

≈ ≈ ≈ ≈ ≈

Do you think the next hominids (if they'll *be* hominids): do you think they'll figure it out? I mean, who could *invent* a story like this? But it's fun to imagine them scratching their heads. They'll examine the artifacts, tracing the past from what remains: the carapace creatures of plastic and metal, with wires for veins and an eye made of glass. They'll surmise it was all a religious ritual. Maybe they're right.

≈ ≈ ≈ ≈ ≈

My daughter sings like a lotus flower: sleep like dreams, narcotic delusion. I can't get the mojo to fear the apocalypse, not when I hear her. But why did Odysseus travel home? I 'murdered' a fetus. I fed my children. To feed my children, farmers sprayed: soft rain came down in the moonlight of chemicals. Maybe a mother was killed by a drone, like a bee or collateral. Naval destroyer: *protect my nephew from the war*. My daughter was chained to the factory floor for the tiniest tank top she wears on the boat. But the cost will be borne by developing countries— storms and flood, or drought and famine. Rafts of people, pitching themselves inside the oceans.

It's three degrees…

It's seventeen years…

It's a thousand lifetimes: only one.

I citrus the orange. It sounds so small. As small as a thumbnail. I'd like three degrees in the middle of winter. The human mind is bleached like coral: brainwash, Clorox, bright so bright against tanned skin. But three degrees is a seismic wave, the kind that glides so smooth in the ocean. It's imperceptible out at sea. It could be here now; we'd never know, except we do. It's caused by trauma: an earthquake or death of a father or child; a landslide or undersea movement of conscience. It's one or the other or maybe it's every. The tipping has come; I can feel its peak. I swear, I can sense it: we're never so close as I am at this moment.

≈ ≈ ≈ ≈ ≈

When I was a child, I'd stand on the shoreline and stare at the waves. Surrounded by that rage—this voracity—I'd beg the ocean to knock me down: *Please, hit me full and hard on the chest.* I desire to be, if I'm pulverized inside that force. You're the only man who understood; you saw me there, alone on the beach. You were curled in the lungs of a humpback whale. You wanted to ocean with all your power, instead you made love. You were always a punk, now you listen to jazz. I will suck on your necklace, tenderly.

≈ ≈ ≈ ≈ ≈

The music stops. It seems very sudden. My daughter keeps singing: such purling voice. She'll lure the soldiers to their slumber. Cradle them sweetly; they'll feel no pain. But jet planes engine toward the suction. Lurch in the wake of this massive ship. From peak to peak, from crest to nipple: thoughts are rising. Now they fall.

Bleed the ethical; blood the orange.

No need to struggle—not anymore.

The decisions are already made.

We 'humans' are no longer class 'Mammalia.' Our species is now geological force. We're unable to octopus what we've released. It's a progress that's natural: don't blame the species. We have big brains, but beastly libidos. We're only an animal. Pity us. We've lost our God.

≈ ≈ ≈ ≈ ≈

The currents of magma determine the earth's magnetic field. They cause the compass to pull directional: race toward the pole and guide me home. My moral compass: iron blood. The pour of amnion. Who will cleanse us? How do we know what's 'right' and 'good' when we don't have a God or a book to declare it? Absolve our sins, absorb our carbon; ride me, steady, through this ocean. I only feel clean when you fuck me.

#29.

A whale dove down, through shallow waters. He dug a piece of shale with his mouth; you wear it around your neck on a chain. It's a fossil whose words are in Hebrew.

≈ ≈ ≈ ≈ ≈

The whale was your father. He grew two blowholes on top of his head. He could breathe through those passages; he was preparing. He knew, more than most, the phrase '*I will die*' is not an abstraction. But what could he do? Fall in love, propose marriage, and have two kids by age twenty-two.

He could teach you a mystery of the ocean.
He won't be around when you're older.

He kept you inside his lungs for years, till the polyp burst inside his brain. You were sleeping when they told you the news. "*Wake up! Wake up! Your dad is dead!*" For years, you're not sure what's a dream and what's real.

≈ ≈ ≈ ≈ ≈

The lessons are not in their natural order. You rubbed the lotion when pain was bad. You knew when flares of illness were coming. You saw his skin flake, his itch gnaw: treatments fail. You would get the water for his pills. *Drink it down.*

≈ ≈ ≈ ≈ ≈

You're six years old. "Listen, sonny boy," your father said. What came next was the wisdom: a truth that's indelible, written on stone over thousands of years. But it couldn't mean anything, not to a boy. It's a pattern of sounds. It's the tone of command: that you understood.

≈ ≈ ≈ ≈ ≈

By the time you were ten, he'd determined which mystery he would teach: the complex song of the humpback whale, which no person actually comprehends.

He knew you could handle it.

You learned his song; you memorized themes. You repeated the notes so that you could retain them. He gave you praise and bought you doughnuts: "Don't tell your mother…" As if this were your deepest secret. He took you to work, where you stood and observed. He constructed houses, drove a convertible. The heart of a whale is the size of a car. You could feel it thump as he took curves fast. With wind in your hair: the humpbacks leap higher than any whale. But no one knows why. They think maybe it soothes them: it cleans the pests that irritate skin. It would flake in your hand. You could tell that it hurt him. It soothed him, the lotion. They might breach for fun.

≈ ≈ ≈ ≈ ≈

Breathing, for whales, is an act of will. It's not automatic. It doesn't just happen. He died at your school. It was 'Back to School Night.' You then walked through the hallways. You thought you were dreaming: *Wake up!*

≈ ≈ ≈ ≈ ≈

At age fourteen, you discover punk. You thrash your tail and strike the water, slap your pecs and smash into others. These whales are aggressive, but only when needed. (You need it when you live on the street.) You're fluking up: you vertical beat then you dive to the bottom. Your mother has had it. She sends you away. You stay submerged for the longest time: he gave you capacity in your lungs. From father to son—that's the path of this knowledge. It's only males who sing this song, and only when they're completely alone.

≈ ≈ ≈ ≈ ≈

After two decades, you want to explore the buried lessons. Tune yourself to spectral peaks, the cluster of formants and wave-form shapes. The scientists cautiously draw conclusions: it's possibly larynx and muscle dynamics, with U-fold vibration and air-filled sacs. In truth, the scientists only guess. This whale is evasive, exceedingly private. He only has time for what's important.

Listen, sonny boy…

You plot, on a graph, all the frequency jumps. They become non-linear: a pattern that's normal for woodwind and brass. You discover jazz. You lie on your bed and remember the phrases. The record plays; you'd memorized themes. The somatic sensations provided feedback. Songs evolve—old patterns discarded, retained like a haunting. You're now thirty-three: the age of your father when he died.

≈ ≈ ≈ ≈ ≈

You come to shore: an awkward boy who'd lived in a whale, who'd learned life's themes before it was natural.

You are an oddity.
I am uneven.

You ride above, along this song you now understand. I'm watching your breathing, your body above me. I wrap my legs around your hips. You like my strength; it poses a challenge. I know what I want. I want leaps that are gorgeous, are violent: non-linear. Hold your hips with the vice of my muscle. I look in your eyes as I draw myself toward you. I take your necklace in my mouth.

Between the teeth, I'll lay myself down.
You will follow.

#30.

'Climatic stimuli' include the tongue. Also the burning of fossil fuels. I've read the books; they're filled with words. But sometimes words don't mean what we think. It depends on my mood. "So… what kind of mood are you in?" you ask. We're lying in bed; I'm reading a book about climate change. Perusing the glossary—'disaster,' 'resistance,' 'vulnerability'— I'm visiting you for the first time in several months. The days abrade; uncertain how to be with each other, we strain against routines and values. Then nights come ('upwelling,' 'risk,' 'transformation'). You want my attention. But I flip the page, determined to stay with the task I've brought.

"How about some jazz?" you ask.

"I need to work."

"So… how about you work while we listen to jazz?"

This moment could go either way; I hesitate. "Let's try it," I say. I return to the glossary… 'Extreme events' are expected to increase, but we'll be provided with 'cultural services': recreation, aesthetic enjoyment, and also (surprisingly) 'spiritual fulfillment.' You look at me quizzically. "Why's that surprising—that 'culture' is spiritual? I'll tell you, babe: this is better than synagogue…" You stand by the records. You're 'vertical column,' six-foot-four. "With jazz," you continue, "you need a guide. You can't learn from a book." It *must* be a person: "A book can only give you words…" "And what will you give?" My determination is starting to wane.

You slip the record from its sleeve.

"Go ahead," you say, removing your shirt…

"I don't mind if you read."

We sex and motor from the coast. At two hundred nautical miles, we pause: we've become 'exclusive.' Your sea levels rise. We submerge in vibration; the record plays. You tell me how to feel the sax—its alto tone—but soon the singer overtakes. A female voice. Her cooler, water, 'welling up'; it's deeper, 'driven toward the surface.' Now our ocean 'overturns.' My hair drapes down. I ease apart, each current of sound. I am seagrass and mangroves. The music glides. You 'dominate regions and wilderness areas, causing a total loss of control.' It's the 'watershed moment.' The glossary tells us: we both require 'immediate response to satisfy critical human needs.'

I'm done with the glossary. Flick the light. The bedroom is midnight. I read the book, but deeper now. I delve inside the Executive Summary. Facts irrefutable: bulleted points making holes in my blood. With statistics, predictions, about the effects of climate change. My mood has shifted.

"What's up?" you say.
"I can't sleep," I reply.

You leave the bed and return to the music. From hundreds of records, you are my guide. "This can help," you say. You can help, if I'll let you. I lay my head on your chest, on your breathing. Before I start speaking my anxious thoughts, the record begins: Lionel Hampton, playing the vibes.

"Can you hear it?" you ask.
But the 'it' isn't specified.

Follow the melody: mallets on the metal bars. My muscles tense in concentration. "Relax," you say. "Relax and listen…" "To *what*?" I ask. But then I sense it: Hampton's voice, far off, in the background. He's humming the notes—but it's barely detectable; it's the ineffable, given to music. "It's kind of like laughter…" You whisper.

Can you hear it, Marianne?
It's kind of like joy.

#31.

Life doesn't disappear, although that's what 'abortion' means. My bible tells me: *ab* + *oriri*—'away' from 'appearing'— becomes *abortare* through frequent, repeated, intensification. She'll never appear through continual effort not to see.

I'd like to abort that conclusion.

≈ ≈ ≈ ≈ ≈

Elision: abortion. What's cut is the tissue—material, body— potential for life. But the potency—energy—gets released. It's hubris to think we could nullify that; it's like saying that humans could kill the earth...

Abortion exists in a realm I call 'spirit.' I can't hold this concept inside my brain. In my womb: then I could, like the hint of a secret whose words I can't know. Only whispers and tingling, like breath on the nape. Like the promise of more. I believe this sensation.

Refracted through the lens of sin, we quickly reach abyssal blue. But light, in the deep, is a radiant body whose warmth fills my veins and my mouth with its song. Luminesce in this lightness: I don't seek forgiveness. I seek, instead, to bear the burden of my awareness.

"Bear it with me," I'll say to you.
Intensely, repeatedly: Bear it with me.

#32.

Carbon dioxide is breaking the bond of word and meaning. The chemists describe it: reactions are faster than Saturday nights at a poetry festival. Link up, break up, rapid-dissolve amidst accusations and hydrogen ions. It's all so predictable: I, too, was an overcharged ion, when I was young. But it can't remain in that free-floating state: it'll bind with reliable carbonate, the conjugal base of carbonic acid. Carbonate ions are highly established; you'll see them in oceans and near the bar. Then high-heeled hydrogen (positive spike as she walks in the room) will unwittingly cause a massive disruption. She's seeking excitement and polar experience. Carbonate ions attempt to keep up, but they'll soon get depleted. Disaster awaits, but the gossip is positively electric.

To put it more plainly...
Within forty years, the pH of oceans will alter the very basis of life.

The chemical cause is carbon dioxide from fossil fuels.
The *actual* cause, of course, is us.

Please: try to take in all the facts.
Absorb them, completely, then hand me the flogger.

I know what you're thinking: self-flagellation is very distasteful.
I think I'll flagellate you instead.

I like that you take it: combining our intimate with a performance. It's very rare. Most large-scale predators are endangered. You lie in bed. The cuffs bind you firmly. You're straining against them; your muscle is iron. You won't submit. It's just like a game, except everything's real.

You can feel the surge of your deep-sea dynamics: your fear or your power; your failure, desire. The pain is as full, but the boundary's clear. You're safe in this bedroom, the size of a fantasy or a book. The world out there: that's a different story.

Whip the bull kelp; mistress and torment. I'll gauge when I've taken you past the point. I'll stay for a moment—*steady, love, although it hurts*—then I ease back. But the gentlest kiss always comes when it's over. The tips of my hair and the leather, like feathers. You're stronger now. You know you'll survive, if only so you'll feel this kiss.

We cannot take this overly seriously: sex and the oceans, which also means love.

There's no possible 'overly' in this case: there's nothing more basic to human life.

But if we can't dissolve the tension, we'll all get brained by the weight of the tuna.

Some people thrive on that kind of anxiety—I once did... But I'll wait over here.

Can you pass me the olives for my martini? Then, if you will: bind my carbon.

#33.

All this time, I had it wrong. Seduce, subduct, erupt with force that mimics depth, but might be youth. We lust pyrotechnic; we acrobatic in downtown bars whose cheap beer smells like poets.

I thought it had to be spectacular.

Write a tsunami. Earthquakes rock and underwater; oceans army like a wall. Or maybe I'll perform a volcano: I'll lava till my throat is raw. They'll hear the bleed in how my pen. My vital pulse is proven.

As it turns out, I was wrong.

The magma that flows through the ocean is fresh. The ridge extends for thousands of miles. The seafloor spreads, but all the movement comes from this: a channel the width of your breath. Inhale deep. The ground is shifting—two slow centimetres every year.

We move the length of a gasp in our lifetime.

This is the opening. Gentle, gently: dilation of souls... In this widening space, I can let words come less violently. Less needful of clinging to wanted conclusions: I try to explain it. This language, creating: this molten core where life becomes, inside my body.

Gentle, gently: you turn away.

#34.

If I look at your heart, I can see it's not red. It's the colour of oceans: that grey-slate scale of blue and salt. I'd wanted to redeem our past, to write the story of our future—love embodied not by *her*, but by the way we've come together. Seal the ending, tighter than I would in a book. I fold my clothes. I tuck away the promises we couldn't keep—the dresses that I didn't wear; the conversations never shared because of the tension. I fold my words inside my throat. I look at you, a man whom I will always love. You sit on the bed and watch me pack: "Don't run away from where you're supposed to be," you say. "You can't do that...

"Not if you want to honour the dead."

≈ ≈ ≈ ≈ ≈

What would've happened if life had been different. If I'd had two fins and you stood nine feet tall. If I'd taken the pill; if we hadn't done ecstasy. *Timothy Leary cancelled the party!* If my shirt were grey or your shoulders less broad. If we hadn't been gleeful that afternoon. "It's love," you said. If we'd taken a moment, and tried to discuss. *Listen, sonny boy...* You listened, I see you, I see how you breathe. If the plates hadn't smashed. If the moon hadn't spun. If the comet hadn't hit the earth. But then comes the twilight, when creatures are luminous. Rise to the boundary when sun has set. The nights are safer. At night, I could let you hold me completely.

At night, I forgot who I'd become.

≈ ≈ ≈ ≈ ≈

She'd be an adult. She'd be young and in love. She'd be making mistakes with a mermaid or sailor. She'd kiss like laughter, lie in the sun as the storm rolls in. She'd hear the blare of crisis and climate. She'd harmonize songs to the humpback whale. Insouciant beauty. The ocean will cool as it swirls at her ankles. I'm watching it happen. I hear her—her voice—as an echo that rushes between the words.

Don't run away...
It doesn't honour the living.

#35.

I'm alone with the book; it's over, again. I'm not sure how it ends. As we split apart, I'll seek the place where we began. I open the dictionary: open, O, I'll start with 'origin.'

My body is lowered through pages of water like language, swirling around my skin. I arrive at the origin—meaning the 'source'— though it also signifies 'coming into being.' Our origin, then, is a place *and* a movement, emerging from the verb 'to rise.'

The source of life—our 'genesis'—is a series of hydrothermal vents: spectacular openings from the core. Ecstatic eruptions, a chaos of heat: in the depths of Oceanic night, the oldest 'original' forms of life don't rely on the sun. They create their own sugars, becoming a body by drawing on infernal fires of magma.

'Magma' comes from the Greek 'to knead,' which leads to 'unguent': salve that's used for soothing and healing. Anoint my skin; it means 'to smear.' You'll cover my body with powdered gold. I'll glisten for you. This is origin, source; it relates to 'surge'— the rolling motion of the ocean, swelling from sources we cannot see. As a noun, it means 'onrush'—a current, electric, that pulses.

Heated by magma, the planet's interior bursts through the vents—a transgression of boundaries that generates life. This boundary is called a 'terminus': the ocean 'de-termines' what life can exist. From beginning to end, since our oceans also 'regulate' climate: a word that means 'rule.' I don't like that word. It feels too governmental, until I discover: to 'regulate' shares its tongue with 'surge.' The ocean will top us from below.

Life began through 'chemosynthesis,' from the Greek: 'to place together, chemically.' I sense you with me; I'm swimming through language. It's gold on my skin; I can feel your hands. I can't understand: this power, potential, was given to us. Like a gift, or an offering. You bring me: that's all an offering ever was. You 'bring me toward,' but I will lead. It's called 'seduction.' This theme becomes an 'embodied perception.' Linguistically, theme can also mean 'stem.' I'll suck its pith, as if that could fulfill me.

'Fate' is merely a 'power or principle which pre-determines': it sets the limit before we begin. I'm approaching that boundary. Our fate has been written: its root is the past, it's the part which means 'speak.' We've been talking for eons, for billions of years, since the shimmer of life started in the sea. Now my mouth is an ocean of words I can't say. How can love remain—although we're surging toward our end? I try to pretend we can stay, as we dream, but the oracle tells us: fate can't be denied. It *can* be ignored, but that'd be stupid. No need to define it.

≈ ≈ ≈ ≈ ≈

Alone with the book; it's over again.
I start with O.

#36.

The only evidence of their existence: a little volcano they leave as they dive. We've spent the day on detritus beach, just Blythe and I. She's played in the ocean, built castles of sand; now we're heading home—but Blythe stops short. She's noticed some motion at her feet. A mound has formed! She steps: two more. She stops.

"Is it magic?"

We crouch together, an intimate breathing. Her hair is wet; the sand grains stick along her legs. My sundress gently tickles my skin. Now the mounds are appearing in solid ground. Intense concentration: our breath is swirling in currents between us. We form a conch, the sound of the sea. Put the image of us to your ear and listen...

Is this sound me, or her, or the ocean?

Blythe stares intently at the sand.

She attempts to make sense of—

Another appears!

I can feel her tension: quiver, happy, through her muscles.

"Mom! There's another!"

"I see it," I whisper. My words are amplified by our closeness.

"Where does it come from?"

"What do you think?"

She's trusting me. She doesn't know. She couldn't possibly: Blythe was only nine weeks' fetal. She's barely the size of the strange little creature that hops on the beach. She's the size of a thumbnail. Her brain is a stem not a mind that can know either pain or betrayal.

Her dad: he's the one who knew.

We walk along the plastic beach. The sand is made from petroleum products: a speck of silver from bags of chips; the greenish zest from bottles of water. "It's almost as nice as the old sand," I say, "the sand that's made from grains of quartz..." (It's important, at this point, to lie to children.) Blythe is burbling. She wants to explain why the mounds appear. She's made a story: they're ancient islands with fires for rituals; maidens are scared at the edge of volcanoes; eruptions of lava since gods are mad.

"Is that why they're there? Is that it? Is it, mom?"

"It could be," I say. I squeeze her hand.

"I knew it!" she says.

It's a civilization inside her mind: a whole huge world with weirdness and order. She sees the fire. I see her eyes. They blaze with reflected light of lava. Blythe is the maiden: she's very romantic, just like her mother. I recognize this lonely child... "We can't see the lava 'cause it's so hot!" She releases my hand to spread her fingers. Taut like lightning, sparks from the tips. She can't contain it. I sense her excitement, her fingers alive as I pen the words. The little girl. The lovely child, never born.

"I'm gonna tell daddy about the volcanoes..."

She turns to me sternly: "Don't tell him, okay?"

"I promise," I answer.

They'll look at the evidence someday, perhaps. They'll create a story from what remains—a narrative of what went wrong. That 'story,' say scientists, might be the methane: a greenhouse gas that poised to pulse. It's locked in the ice—in the Arctic tundra—stable since the Permian Era. But that ice is melting.

'*Permafrost*' is no longer permanent.
Even our language can't keep up.

I look at the mounds spread across the sand. I know the cause: a shrimp-like crustacean without a shell. It lives beneath the rotting kelp. These amphipods hop, and the methane will pulse, but the people on detritus beach don't see it. They thought it was all a wonderful fiction.

#37.

All that remains when we die is a poem.

The weight and heat of our lives press down. The pressure transforms us. My body, in time, will become this potency: one small poem. That's all I get.

I'd like to live it well.

We met in the starlight when planets were forming. I will not meet him until tomorrow. We'll make a child who won't be born.

The girl with the freckles has large brown eyes.

They're deep like woods, like trees cut down.

It's only males who sing this song, and only when they're completely alone.

Only whispers and tingling, like breath on the nape. Like the promise of more. I believe this sensation.

The afterbirth is the expulsion of the placenta. The placenta is an organ attached to the lining of your womb during pregnancy. It keeps your unborn baby's blood supply separate from your own blood supply, as well as providing a link between the two. The link allows the placenta to carry out functions that your unborn baby can't perform for itself.

FURTHER READING

"Mama?"

Scientific data increasingly support the claim that the earth has entered the sixth extinction. One recent study which encapsulates this theory is worth quoting at length:

> The evidence is incontrovertible that recent extinction rates are unprecedented in human history and highly unusual in Earth's history. Our analysis emphasizes that our global society has started to destroy species of other organisms at an accelerating rate, initiating a mass extinction episode unparalleled for 65 million years. If the currently elevated extinction pace is allowed to continue, humans will soon (in as little as three human lifetimes) be deprived of many biodiversity benefits. On human time scales, this loss would be effectively permanent because in the aftermath of past mass extinctions, the living world took hundreds of thousands to millions of years to rediversify (Ceballos et al.).

In this piece, I use the statistic that 75% of current species will become extinct. This is an extrapolation. As the study states: "Although biologists cannot say precisely how many species there are, or exactly how many have gone extinct in any time interval, we can confidently conclude that modern extinction rates are exceptionally high, that they are increasing, and that they suggest a mass extinction is under way— the sixth of its kind in Earth's 4.5 billion years of history" (Ceballos et al.). I derived my extrapolation in this way:

• In the previous five extinctions, a loss of 60–70% of all species was minimum, with the 'Great Dying' of the Permian era killing 90% of all species.
• We're headed toward those rates of extinction. The work of Todd Palmer, a professor of biology at the University of Florida (and one of the researchers on the study cited above) is discussed in the *Washington Post*: "If die-offs continue at current rates, the current extinction event could reach 'Big Five' magnitudes in 240 to 540 years, [Palmer] said—an unprecedented speed for this kind of ecological change" (Kaplan).

• I therefore chose a number between 60 and 90%. Specifically, I use the phrase "three-quarters of all species will be dead."

We danced beneath palm trees whose fronds are pink and blue
Nitrogen fertilizers, as applied in large-scale agriculture, are significantly altering marine ecosystems. Runoff chokes the ocean by artificially stimulating the reproduction of phytoplankton, which then dies and gets decomposed by bacteria—a process which depletes the ocean of oxygen, creating 'dead zones' that are literally devoid of life (Mitchell, 44–5). I discuss this phenomenon more extensively below, in the note to 'The ocean releases its breath like a gift.'

Coral reefs have become a stark illustration of climate change, with vibrant reefs replaced by ghostly, calcified landscapes. Given that 80% of Caribbean reefs are already dead, and Pacific reefs are increasingly under threat, scientists have initiated efforts at "assisted evolution." Through this strategy, scientists are genetically engineering wild species to enable them to withstand the effects of human behaviour. Researchers at the Hawaii Institute of Marine Biology are attempting to locate—and then breed—the coral that's best able to thrive in warmer temperatures (Kolbert, 2016). This, perhaps, is the end of the human industrial revolution: we are starting to engineer life on earth.

"Mama, where does the ocean come from?"
Scientists aren't certain about the origin of the ocean. Theories are discussed in *Ocean* by Sylvia Earle and Linda Glover. They're also summarized by Tobias C. Owen of the Institute for Astronomy in Honolulu, Hawaii, using a richness of scientific language:

> There are basically three possible sources for the water. It could have (1) separated out from the rocks that make up the bulk of the earth; (2) arrived as part of a late-accreting veneer of water-rich meteorites, similar to the carbonaceous chondrites that we see today; or (3) arrived as part of a late-accreting veneer of icy planetesimals, that is, comets.

My nephew was drowned as a Navy SEAL but now he's beside me, face down in the water

At the end of the First Gulf War, Saddam Hussein ordered his army to set fire to Kuwaiti oil fields. The blaze lasted eight months, longer than the war itself. The Iraqi army also dumped ten million barrels of oil into the sea. "There were fires shooting out of the ground for as far as I could see. It was like the end of the world," says photographer Steve McCurry (Canby). McCurry is best known for his photograph "Afghan Girl," which appeared on the cover of *National Geographic* in 1984. Images from the Kuwaiti blazes, as well as McCurry's other work, can be found on his website.

San Diego Harbor is shared by the U.S. Naval Base San Diego and U.S. Customs and Border Protection, which inspects vessels bringing agriculture into the country from abroad. The environmental impact of shipping—an industry which sustains our consumptions habits—is due to three main factors: tankers' air pollution; accident spills (and deliberate discharges) of oil and chemicals; and the dumping of waste directly into the ocean. Science writer Fred Pearce makes this graphic comparison: "Just 16 of the world's largest ships can produce as much lung-clogging sulphur pollution as all the world's cars" (2009). Yet there are over 100,000 such ships in our oceans.

He rarely calls me by my name

The Mariana Trench, located in the Pacific Ocean, is the deepest place in the ocean, reaching a depth of almost 11,000 metres. The 'Ring of Fire' is a horseshoe-shaped area in the Pacific basin, correlated to the location of tectonic plates. Over 90% of earthquakes and 75% of volcanoes occur along the Ring of Fire, hence its name. The cucumber referenced in the piece is a *sea* cucumber (a soft-bodied echinoderm), not a wayward vegetable.

Seagrass spreads in the Mediterranean, beds of fronds and roots like ginger

'Oceanic time lag' is a simple concept with immense implications. "The time lag occurs because rising air temperatures take time to make themselves felt throughout the immense thermal mass of the oceans. This 'thermal inertia' means that Earth has not yet felt the full effect of today's level of greenhouse gases, explains [Gerald] Meehl," a climatologist at the U.S. National Center for Atmospheric Research (Holmes). That 'full effect'—the impact on temperature, sea-level rise, and consequent phenomena—won't be felt for at least a century (Holmes; Watson et al.). In other words, the distance between 'cause' and 'effect' is 100 years, a timespan that masks the consequences of our actions.

This lag is especially significant, since the ocean absorbs 93% of "additional heating produced and accumulated by global warming" (Reid, 23)—heat which will be released long after carbon emissions are reduced. "We perhaps haven't realised the gross effect we are having on the oceans, we don't appreciate what they do for us," says Dan Laffoley, a marine adviser to the International Union for Conservation of Nature (IUCN) (Milman). If the heat absorbed by the oceans were, instead, absorbed by the atmosphere, earth's temperature would've warmed by 36° Celsius in the past half century—an unthinkable number. As stated in a recent report by the IUCN: "Whether ocean warming impacts a particular group of organisms, alters the structures of ecosystems such as coral reefs, changes the very essence of environmental conditions, or indeed influences weather, it impacts everyone to some degree as we are an ocean planet" (Lundin and Laffoley, 8).

Time lag, however, isn't limited to ocean ecosystems. A report by the Intergovernmental Panel on Climate Change (IPCC) focuses on the "inertia" in climate systems *and* human systems (i.e., in the ability of governments and individuals to change their behaviour). The language involutes; those spirals serve to amplify the urgency of the message:

> Inertia is a widespread inherent characteristic of the interacting climate, ecological, and socio-economic systems. Thus some impacts of anthropogenic climate change may be slow to become apparent, and some could be irreversible if climate change is not limited in both rate and magnitude before associated thresholds, whose positions may be poorly known, are crossed (Watson et al.).

There's no illumination here

Since their discovery in 1977, hydrothermal vents have changed our understanding of how life originated on earth. Essentially, microbes utilized chemicals to form sugar. The chemicals are dissolved in the superheated water, which reaches 400° Celsius—almost as hot as the surface of Venus. The core of earth served, in a way, as a substitute for the sun—as if the sun were internal to the body of earth, providing the heat necessary to convert energy into matter.

Various websites provide recordings of undersea phenomena. To hear the hydrothermal vents—in addition to whales singing, lightning as it penetrates water, magma seeping, seals trilling—I recommend two websites: Discovery of Sound in the Sea (DOSITS), developed by the University of Rhode Island's Graduate School of Oceanography in partnership with Marine Acoustics, Inc.; and the National Oceanic and Atmospheric Administration (NOAA) of the U.S. government (see its gallery of ocean sounds). Videos of the vents are available on the website of the Woods Hole Oceanographic Institution.

The ocean releases its breath like a gift

Scientists estimate that phytoplankton contribute 50 to 85% of oxygen in the earth's atmosphere. 'Ghost fishing' occurs when lost or abandoned fishing gear traps fish and mammals, which eventually die as they float, captured, through the water. At this point, it's hard to know the extent of the problem (Smith), although it's undoubtedly dwarfed by bycatch—i.e., fish that are inadvertently caught by trawlers and nets. The World Wildlife Federation (WWF) estimates that bycatch constitutes 40% of global marine catches (Davies et al.). Most bycatch is thrown back into the water, either dead or wounded.

In this piece, I mention in passing the "column of water that's void of life." Here, I'm referring to the 'dead zones.' These are expanses of water where oxygen is severely depleted. This condition, known as hypoxia, kills whatever life exists in that zone, and causes other animals to skirt around the area, as if encountering a physical boundary. There are approximately 400 dead zones in the world (Diaz et al.); the largest is in the Gulf of Mexico, where the dead zone is the size of New Jersey. Conditions are so poor in the Gulf because it serves as the drainage basin for the Mississippi River, which carries chemical fertilizers and nutrients from farmland along its length. On its website, the NOAA describes the phenomenon in dispassionate terms:

nutrient pollution is the primary cause of those zones created by humans. Excess nutrients that run off land or are piped as wastewater into rivers and coasts can stimulate an overgrowth of algae, which then sinks and decomposes in the water. The decomposition process consumes oxygen and depletes the supply available to healthy marine life (NOAA).

More evocative is a statement by Dan Leonard, owner of a clam farm in the Gulf of Mexico:

> Nutrients flowing into the gulf are killing life here, creating red tides and a huge dead zone where nothing can live. The water has next to no oxygen. Every summer, the dead zone grows, snuffing out more fish, crabs, and other animals. And we're the perpetrators of the crime, with our excess fertilizer and untreated sewage and other waste flowing into the gulf. The dead zone, once unheard of, is starting to kill everything in its path. In spring when I'm in the water tending my clam beds, I can almost feel it coming (Dybas).

My blood contains one drop of molten, gold from when the earth was formed
Light and sound function differently in the ocean than on land. This piece fleetingly mentions various phenomena such as Snell's window (whereby the entire sky is framed by a small 'window' when one looks upward while submerged—and whose shattering causes the distinctive scintillation on the water's surface); the polarization of light in saltwater; the blueness of the ocean; and the bioluminescence of fish in the Midnight Zone (the deepest of the three oceanic zones—a place where sunlight cannot penetrate). Varying speeds of sound within the ocean—speeds which are altered by temperature and pressure—cause the unusual sonic contours which humans experience when underwater. This information is readily available, but I recommend the data presented by the Woods Hole Oceanographic Institute (Sosik and Johnsen) and *Deep Sea News* (Martini).

Maybe we shouldn't have been so gleeful, but we couldn't help it: we ate avocados that afternoon
In 1969, an oil spill off the coast of Santa Barbara, California, rallied the nascent environmental movement. The outcry led to various foundational pieces of environmental legislation, and to the birth of

Earth Day (Easton). The 'relics' imagined at the natural-medicine store are all *actual* casualties of continued oil spills off Santa Barbara.

My writing on mating rituals was informed by Alanna Mitchell's book *Sea Sick* (100-121) as well as the internet, which is rife with bizarre mating behaviours of all species (including those that live in the ocean).

The decision was mutual

Although the issue of sanitation isn't "sexy," as one research put it, it's vital for protecting the health of people and ecosystems (Pappas). Currently, 2.6 billion people lack adequate sanitation, meaning 90% of sewage is dumped directly into the water (Pappas). The issue will only get worse with climate change, as storm surges increase in frequency and intensity. These surges result in the dumping of untreated waste, as heavy rainfall overwhelms sanitation infrastructure. This is already occurring in both the developing *and* the developed world.

Inadequate filtration at sanitation plants is also causing "hormonal pollution," which stems from birth control pills. Given that up to 68% of each dose of oral contraceptives is released from the body (Fears)—and that water filtration plants don't remove these chemicals (Thomson)— fish and amphibians are basically taking constant doses of estrogen. The result is reproductive abnormalities, either through sterilization or the creation of intersex fish and amphibians. In one study, fertilization rates decreased by 30% in two generations of Japanese medaka fish (Fears); in another, male fish started to produce eggs (Thomson).

He'd held my hand in the waiting room

The same acoustic principles operate for three diverse phenomena: biosonar in whales and dolphins, medical ultrasound machines, and military submarines. The history of these phenomena is interlinked. Various countries developed sonar during the First and Second World Wars, spurred by a need to detect enemy submarines and underwater mines. The concept for this technology was based on observation of biosonar in bats and cetaceans. Military technology was then repurposed for civilian use, primarily in medicine, with ultrasound machines. Now, the military's sonar is causing distress to cetaceans: beaked and blue whales are avoiding the sound, which leads to interruptions of feeding and mating patterns, as well as several mass strandings (Carrington).

They hovered in white gowns and white sheets, a wonderland of ghostly fluorescence

My information about fish sleep was culled from various sources spread throughout books and the internet; my information on the relationship between anesthesia and sleep derives from one primary article, "Learning and Memory during Sleep and Anesthesia" (Reasor and Poe).

The phrase 'sixth extinction' was popularized by American journalist Elizabeth Kolbert, who writes about this phenomenon in her book *The Sixth Extinction: An Unnatural History*. Jan Zalasiewizc, professor of paleobiology at the University of Leicester, explains the situation succinctly: "We are now living through one of those brief, rare episodes in Earth history when the biological framework of life is dismantled" (Zalasiewizc). I discuss this phenomenon more extensively above, in the note to *"Mama?"*.

Tectonic plates glide over skeletal remains

"The continental plates float on calcium carbonate, much of it from vast collections of subocean microbial skeletons," according to evolutionary theorist Lynn Margulis and writer Dorion Sagan (Earle and Glover, 58). The book in which their essay can be found, *Ocean: An Illustrated Atlas*, also contains a section 'Categories of Life in the Sea' (71-81) which includes a description of oceanic fungi, plants, animals, and worms.

If he was there, I don't recall

Although popular culture tends to focus on the melting of ice sheets in Greenland, the loss of glaciers in Alaska is causing equal damage to the environment (Chapin et al., 519). Alaska is warming twice as fast as the rest of the United States; this is particularly dangerous, since the state has reserves of some of the largest glaciers on earth, pouring 40–70 gigatons of melted ice into the oceans each year (Chapin, 516 and 519).

Sea levels are currently the highest ever recorded, according to the NOAA. In 2015, the average global sea level was 2.75 inches higher than in 1993, the year when satellite measurements began (Blunden and Arndt, S80-81). Sea-level rise is already causing the disappearance of low-lying Pacific islands: five have disappeared, with six others experiencing "severe shoreline recession," which has necessitated the relocation of various communities (Simon et al.).

Maybe he lived in a mangrove forest

The quotations (sort of) attributed to the musician at the Vancouver Folk Festival—statistics about the effects of climate change in Africa— come from the Intergovernmental Panel on Climate Change (IPCC); these were published as part of a 2007 fact sheet which begins with this statement: "No continent will be struck as severely by the impacts of climate change as Africa" (AMCEN Secretariat). Eight years later, at the Paris Conference on Climate Change, African countries presented a unified vision of the continent's approach to the issue through the Conference of African Heads of State on Climate Change. This group advocated for increased development of renewable resources (which Africa has in abundance), while also urging Western countries to invest in the continent. The African delegation highlighted the political issue at the core of current global negotiations (Adesina), namely: How will developed countries, which have benefited from centuries of greenhouse-gas emissions that fuelled their economies, support developing countries to prosper without exacerbating climate change?

Mangrove forests are increasingly under threat due to logging, overfishing, pollution and climate change (Daru et al.). The mangroves in Senegal are no exception: "In a few decades, Senegal has lost 40% of its mangrove surface," according to Haïdar El-Ali, the Senegalese Minister of Ecology and the Environment (Arthus-Bertrand and Skerry, 98).

The glorious union of death and fuck was never so obvious as in a salmon

Salmon return to their natal waters—sometimes travelling thousands of miles—by following the earth's magnetic fields. In addition, the smell of their birthplace is imprinted strongly when they set out as juveniles; this may help to guide them home (Putnam et al.). Salmon physiology changes dramatically in the fish's all-encompassing focus on return and reproduction. Of course, salmon don't actually 'fuck,' per se. Instead, the female digs a nest in the gravel, using her tail; she then signals that she's ready by tapping her anal fin, at which point the male salmon compete for dominance; when the winner joins the female, they'll hover side by side, simultaneously releasing their eggs and sperm into the nest. Many subspecies of salmon are currently endangered.

Saturday night and the internet calls

Overfishing has become a dire problem, with 80% of the world's fisheries either fully exploited or over exploited according to the

United Nations (Resumed Review Conference). Only 10% of large, predatory fish remain in the oceans as compared to pre-industrial levels (Myers and Worm, 280). With technological advances in ships, gear, and fish-finding equipment, industrial fishers can haul in larger catches and trawl in deeper waters (Tanzer et al., 26). Increasingly, they're 'fishing down'—i.e., seeking species lower down the food web, with effects that ripple through the ocean ecosystem (Earle and Glover, 313). By removing vast numbers of fish from the ocean, we're affecting the ability of those ecosystems to regenerate, leading to what's called 'collapse.'

Taste comes from the core of earth
An extensive discussion of the saltiness of seawater can be found in "Why is the Ocean Salty?" by Herbert Swenson. Originally published by the U.S. Geological Survey, this publication is now online.

I saw you at your wedding
Gravitational forces compete with centrifugal forces, affected by the rotation and orbit of various celestial bodies—sun, moon, and earth—to cause the tides. The physics is described by spring tides, neap tides, apogees, syzygies, culminations; 'harmonic constituents,' bathymetrics and lunations.

Tsunamis are sometimes 'tidal waves,' but that's a misnomer: tsunamis have nothing to do with the tides. Instead, they're caused by underwater earthquakes and volcanoes. Their average height is 100 feet as they approach land; in the deeper ocean, their speed can reach 800 kilometres per hour—the same as an airplane. Despite this speed, tsunamis are often undetected at sea: their energy isn't converted into height until they encounter the shallow waters of the coast.

I crawl in the shell of a horseshoe crab
The Anthropocene is a proposed geological epoch describing the new condition of earth: namely, a condition in which humankind has encroached on virtually all natural processes. That's a layman's definition; a geologist's definition, by contrast, asks "Whether humans have changed the Earth system sufficiently to produce a stratigraphic signature in sediments and ice that is distinct from that of the Holocene epoch" (Waters et al.). The concept was popularized in 2000 by Nobel Prize–winning atmospheric chemist Paul Crutzen. Although the terms is gaining traction

within the wider culture, it hasn't yet been officially accepted among geologists. That may change by the end of this decade: in August 2016, the Anthropocene Working Group made a formal recommendation urging the International Union of Geological Sciences to declare the existence of the Anthropocene (Amos). This decision is not without controversy. Stan Finney, professor at California State University, Long Beach, and chair of the International Commission on Stratigraphy, states: "What you see here is, it's become a political statement. That's what so many people want" (Montaresky). Indeed, even some of the scientists supporting the declaration point toward the practical consequences of the move:

> Formalization is a complex question because, unlike with prior subdivisions of geological time, the potential utility of a formal Anthropocene reaches well beyond the geological community. It also expresses the extent to which humanity is driving rapid and widespread changes to the Earth system that will variously persist and potentially intensify into the future (Waters et al.).

The Working Group must now propose a date at which the Anthropocene began. Possibilities include the beginning of the Industrial Era, with the rise of carbon dioxide, or the dawn of the Atomic Age, which is linked with the 'Great Acceleration' in which changes wrought by humans are happening at an increasingly rapid pace (Amos; Montaresky).

Information about horseshoe crab anatomy comes from the website The Horseshoe Crab, administered by the Ecological Research & Development Group, a non-profit wildlife conservation organization focused on the species.

Soon we'll all be hoarding the ocean; we'll store it in cars so that we can wash them

The number 'three degrees' has come to signify the point we can't cross if we want to avoid catastrophic and irreversible climate change. Scientifically, this number refers to the increase in global average temperature, measured on the Celsius scale, above pre-industrial levels. *Politically*, this term's significance—and the import of holding the line far below that number—is encapsulated by IPCC co-chair Thomas Stocker: "The power of the 2°C target is that it is pragmatic, simple and straightforward to understand and communicate, all important elements when science is brought to policymakers" (Carbon Brief staff). The difficulty that governments face in confronting problems of a planetary nature is epitomized, to me, by that statement.

This piece also alludes to the Deepwater Horizon oil spill in the Gulf of Mexico, the largest marine oil spill in history, which poured 130 million gallons of oil into the Gulf in 2010—some of which remains on the seafloor—and left 4.6 million pounds of oily matter on Louisiana's beaches.

'Environmental migrants'—those "rafts of people" referenced in the piece—is a term proposed by the International Organization for Migration to describe people fleeing their homes due to catastrophic and/or long-term climactic changes, including droughts, flood, soil degradation, and sea-level rise (Mahnke). Other proposed terms are 'climate refugee' or 'climate migrant.' The Internal Displacement Monitoring Centre (IDMC) estimates that 26.4 million people have been displaced from their homes every year since 2008 due to "disasters brought on by natural hazards" (Yonetani et al.).

A whale dove down, through shallow waters
Scientists don't fully understand the acoustic science of whale song—largely because it's challenging to study a muscular creature who's the size of a bus, weighing forty tons, and travelling 5,000 kilometres in a single mating season. In short, humpbacks have eluded us.

The internet is filled with general information about whale song, including haunting audio. Bioacoustics scientist Eduardo Mercado has conducted a detailed, original analysis; he and his colleagues write, "Knowing how a species physically produces sounds can thus provide a useful foundation for understanding the functions that vocalizations may serve" (Mercado et al., 2678).

'Climatic stimuli' include the tongue
The glossary from which I culled language for this piece is included in the report *Oceans and Marine Resources in a Changing Climate* (Griffis and Howard, xix–xxi).

Carbon dioxide is breaking the bond of word and meaning
Ocean acidification is one of the three main effects of anthropogenic climate change on the oceans—the other two are temperature rise and sea-level rise—but the term wasn't even coined until 2003. It refers to the increased pH levels of ocean water.

The cause of acidification is the burning of fossil fuels. The ocean absorbs approximately 25% of carbon dioxide released into the atmosphere (Smithsonian Institute). Acidification primarily affects creatures whose shells are made of calcium carbonate, such as oysters and mussels. Through a chemical chain reaction, they can't extract enough carbonate to build and repair their shells.

The same holds true for corals, which are hit by various forces at once: acidification, which hampers their ability to build their skeleton; overfishing; and (most importantly) temperature rise, which kills the organisms living symbiotically inside them, and whose absence causes coral bleaching.

More dynamic (and potentially catastrophic) is acidification's effect on zooplankton. Not only are these tiny organisms at the base of the food chain, they're also a key component of the 'carbon sink' phenomenon, whereby carbon gets removed from the atmosphere, stored at the bottom of the ocean. Scientists have played out various scenarios through complex models, but haven't arrived at a consensus about the consequences.

Extensive and accessible discussions can be found on the website for the Smithsonian Institute, as well as in Alanna Mitchell's book *Sea Sick*, especially the chapter "Reading the vital signs: pH" (67–81).

All this time, I had it wrong

Maria Tharp was a geologist, cartographer and oceanographic pioneer who mapped the seafloor in the latter half of the twentieth century. By using rudimentary instruments—an echo sounder, ocean-bottom camera, and corer—Tharp and her collaborator, Bruce Heezen, created a topography of the ocean floor. Before them, those contours were utterly unknown (Earle and Glover, 32-33).

Tharp's achievements resulted in further advances that radically altered our understanding of earth's geography. Namely, by depicting the great ridges in the ocean basins—ridges which aligned with areas of seismic activity—she presented a map which led directly to the theories of plate tectonics and continental drift. And she achieved all this while facing intense gender discrimination within the scientific community.

The only evidence of their existence: a little volcano they leave as they dive

Some scientists warn that methane gas—a greenhouse gas that's far more potent than carbon dioxide—could be released in a sudden, massive pulse. The predictions are based on the rapid melting of permafrost, which currently holds a fifty-gigaton reservoir of methane (Whiteman et al.). Such a release would accelerate global warming, exacerbating the effects of glacial melt, sea-ice retreat, sea-level rise, etc. Not all scientists accept this theory, however (Ahmed). Despite the inconclusiveness of the data, what *is* definitive is the extreme climate catastrophe that would result from such a pulse: "Methane heats the atmosphere with an efficiency 25 times that of carbon dioxide, and its release could put in motion a positive feedback loop in which warming releases methane, causing further warming, which liberates even more of the gas" (Mascarelli). Indeed, methane has been implicated in previous global-warming events, including the mass extinction of the Permian Age (Ahmed; Dunham).

In 2009, a 'plastic soup' was discovered in the North Pacific Gyre by Charles Moore, an oceanologist and founder of Algalita Marine Research Foundation. Since then, the problem of oceanic plastic pollution has become a major area of study (Cressey). It's estimated that anywhere from 4.8 million to 12.7 million tons of plastic leak into the ocean each year (Jambek et al.; World Economic Forum, 17). Given that 150 million tons already swirl in our seas, the ocean will contain more plastic than fish by 2050, as measured by weight (World Economic Forum, 17).

Researchers are only now beginning to study the effects of plastic ingestion on marine life (Cressey). One recent study found fertility problems in Pacific oysters exposed to microplastics: 41% fewer larvae were produced by oysters exposed to water with plastic concentrations similar to those found in nature, as opposed to a control group (Sussarellu et al.). Amidst a wealth of complex technical information, the authors of that study write, quite plainly:

Plastics are a contaminant of emerging concern accumulating in marine ecosystems. Plastics tend to break down into small particles, called microplastics, which also enter the marine environment directly as fragments from a variety of sources, including cosmetics, clothing, and industrial processes. Given their ubiquitous nature and small dimensions, the ingestion and impact of microplastics on marine life are a cause for concern, notably for filter feeders" (Sussarellu et al.).

The amphipod who leaves those mounds is sometimes called a sand hopper.

WORKS CITED

Adesina, Akinwumi. "Africa means business on global warming—does the rest of the world?" *The Guardian* (online), Dec 4, 2015.

African Ministerial Conference on Environment (AMCEN) Secretariat. "Climate Change in Africa—What is at Stake? Excerpts from IPCC Reports, the Convention, & BAP." Geneva: Intergovernmental Panel on Climate Change (IPCC), 2007.

Ahmed, Nafeez. "Seven facts you need to know about the Arctic methane timebomb." *The Guardian* (online), Aug 5, 2013.

Amos, Jonathan. "Geologists search for Anthropocene 'golden spike'." *BBC News* (online), Aug 31, 2016.

Arthus-Bertrand, Yann and Brian Skerry. *Man and Sea: Planet Ocean.* New York: Abrams, 2013.

Blunden, J., and D. S. Arndt, eds. "2016: State of the Climate in 2015" Special supplement of the *Bulletin of the American Meteorological Society* 97, no. 8 (Aug 2016). See also accompanying press highlights.

Canby, Thomas. Photographs by S. McCurry. "The Persian Gulf: After the Storm." *National Geographic* 180, no. 2 (Aug 1991): 3–33.

Carbon Brief staff. "Two degrees: The history of climate change's speed limit." *Carbon Brief* (online), Dec 8, 2014.

Carrington, Damian. "Whales flee from military sonar leading to mass strandings, research shows." *The Guardian* (online), Jul 3, 2013.

Ceballos, Gerardo et al. "Accelerated modern human–induced species losses: Entering the sixth mass extinction." *Science Advances* 1, no. 5 (Jun 2015).

Chapin, F. Stuart, III, et al. "Chapter 22: Alaska." In *Climate Change Impacts in the United States: The Third National Climate Assessment,* edited by J. M. Melillo et al., 514–526. Washington, DC: U.S. Global Change Research Program, 2014.

Cressey, Daniel. "Bottles, bags, ropes and toothbrushes: The struggle to track ocean plastics." *Nature* 536 (Aug 2016): 263–65.

Daru B. H. et al. "A Global trend towards the loss of evolutionarily unique species in mangrove ecosystems." *PLoS ONE* 8, no. 6 (Jun 2013).

Davies, R.W.D. et al. "Defining and estimating global marine fisheries bycatch." *Marine Policy* (2009).

Diaz, Robert, and Rutger Rosenberg. "Spreading dead zones and consequences for marine ecosystems." *Science* 321, no. 5891 (Aug 2008): 926–29.

Dunham, Will. "Methane-spewing microbe blamed in earth's worst mass extinction." *Scientific American* (Mar 31, 2014).

Dybas, Cheryl Lyn. "Dead Zones Spreading in World Oceans." *BioScience* 55, no. 7 (2005): 552–57.

Earle, Sylvia A., and Linda K. Glover. *Ocean: An Illustrated Atlas.* Washington, DC: National Geographic Society, 2009.

Easton, Robert O. *Black tide: The Santa Barbara Oil Spill and Its Consequences.* New York: Delacorte Press, 1972.

Fears, Darryl. "Fish don't want birth control, but scientists say they get it from your pill." *The Washington Post* (online), Mar 30, 2015.

Griffis, Roger, and Jennifer Howard, eds. *Oceans and Marine Resources in a Changing Climate: A Technical Input to the 2013 National Climate Assessment.* Washington, DC: Island Press, 2013.

Holmes, Bob. "Ocean heat store makes climate change inevitable." *New Scientist* 17 (Mar 17, 2005).

Jambeck, Jenna R. et al. "Plastic waste inputs from land into the ocean." *Science* 347, no. 6223 (Feb 2015): 768–71.

Kaplan, Sarah. "Earth is on brink of a sixth mass extinction, scientists say, and it's humans' fault." *The Washington Post* (online), Jun 22, 2015.

Kolbert, Elizabeth. *The Sixth Extinction: An Unnatural History.* New York: Henry Holt, 2014.

Kolbert, Elizabeth. "Unnatural Selection." *The New Yorker* (online), Apr 18, 2016.

Lundin, Carl G., and Dan Laffoley. "Preface." In *Explaining Ocean Warming: Causes, Scale, Effects and Consequences,* edited by D. Laffoley and J. M. Baxter, 8–9. Gland, Switzerland: International Union for Conservation of Nature (ICUN), 2016.

Mahnke, Eva. "Climate migration 'a complex problem'." *Our World* (online)/ United Nations University, Oct 31, 2013.

Martini, Kim. "Bending sound: The weird path of sound in the ocean." *Deep Sea News* (online), Oct 10, 2012.

Mascarelli, Amanda Leigh. "A sleeping giant?" *Nature Reports Climate Change* 3 (Apr 2009): 46–9.

Mercado, Eduardo et al. "Sound production by singing humpback whales." *Journal of the Acoustical Society of America* 127, no. 4 (Apr 2010): 2678–91.

Milman, Oliver. "Soaring ocean temperature is 'greatest hidden challenge of our generation'." *The Guardian* (online), Sept 5, 2015.

Mitchell, Alanna. *Sea Sick: The Global Ocean in Crisis.* Toronto: McClelland & Stewart, 2009.

Montaresky, Richard. "Anthropocene: The human age." *Nature* 519 (Mar 2015): 145–47.

Myers, Ransom A., and Boris Worm. "Rapid worldwide depletion of predatory fish communities." *Nature* 423 (May 2003): 280–83.

National Oceanic and Atmospheric Administration (NOAA), National Ocean Service. "What is a dead zone?" NOAA website.

Owen, Tobias. C. "What do we know about the origin of the earth's oceans?" *Scientific American* (online), Oct 21, 1999.

Pappas, Stephanie. "With 7 billion people, world has a poop problem." *Live Science* (online), Oct 25, 2011.

Pearce, Fred. "How 16 ships create as much pollution as all the cars in the world." *Daily Mail* (London), Nov 21, 2009.

Pearlman, Jonathan. "'Oldest living thing on earth' discovered." *The Telegraph* (London), Feb 7, 2012.

Putnam, Nathan F. et al. "Evidence for geomagnetic imprinting as a homing mechanism in pacific salmon." *Current Biology* 23, no. 4 (Feb 2013): 312–16.

Reasor, Jonathan, and G. Poe. "Learning and memory during sleep and anesthesia." *International Anesthesiology Clinics* 64, no. 3 (Summer 2008): 105–29.

Reid, Philip C. "Ocean Warming: Setting the scene." In *Explaining Ocean Warming: Causes, Scale, Effects and Consequences*, edited by D. Laffoley and J. M. Baxter, 17–46. Gland, Switzerland: International Union for Conservation of Nature (ICUN), 2016.

Resumed Review Conference on the Agreement Relating to the Conservation and Management of Straddling Fish Stock and Highly Migratory Fish Stocks. "Fact Sheet: General facts regarding world fisheries." Geneva: United Nations, May 2010.

Simon, Albert et al. "Interactions between sea-level rise and wave exposure on reef island dynamics in the Solomon Islands." *Environmental Research Letters* 11, no. 5 (May 2016).

Smith, Andrew. "Issues Fact Sheet: World inventory of fisheries. Ghost fishing." Geneva: United Nations Food and Agriculture Organization (FAO), Fisheries and Aquaculture Department, May 27, 2005.

Smithsonian Institute, the Ocean Portal Team, reviewed by Jennifer Bennett. "Ocean Acidification." Smithsonian Institute (online).

Sosik, Heidi M., and S. Johnsen. "Shedding light on light in the ocean: New research is illuminating an optically complex environment." *Oceanus Magazine* 43, no. 2 (Dec 2004).

Sussarellu, R. et al. "Oyster reproduction is affected by exposure to polystyrene microplastics." *Proceedings of the National Academy of Sciences* 113, no. 9 (Feb 2016): 2430–35.

Swenson, Herbert. "Why is the ocean salty?" U.S. Geological Survey (online). Originally published 1983 by the U.S. Department of the Interior.

Tanzer, John et al., eds. *Living Blue Planet Report: Species, habitats and human well-being*. Gland, Switzerland: World Wildlife Federation International, 2015.

Thomson, Aly. "Birth control pill threatens fish populations." *CBC News* (online), Oct 13, 2014.

Waters, Colin N. et al. "The Anthropocene is functionally and stratigraphically distinct from the Holocene." *Science* 351, no. 6269 (Jan 2016).

Watson, T. T. and Core Writing Team of IPCC, 2001. *Climate Change 2001: Synthesis Report. A Contribution of Working Groups I, II and III to the Third Assessment Report of the Intergovernmental Panel on Climate Change.* Cambridge: Cambridge University Press, 2001. Question Five, 87–96.

Whiteman, Gail et al. "Climate science: Vast costs of Arctic change." *Nature* 499, no. 7459 (Jul 2013): 401–03.

World Economic Forum. *The New Plastics Economy — Rethinking the future of plastics.* Isle of Wight: Ellen MacArthur Foundation and McKinsey & Company, 2016.

Yonetani, Michelle et al. *Global Estimates 2015: People displaced by disasters.* Geneva: Internal Displacement Monitoring Centre, 2015.

Zalasiewizc, Jan. "The earth stands on the brink of its sixth mass extinction and the fault is ours." *The Guardian* (online), Jun 21, 2015.

The epigraphs for parts one and two—the First and Second Trimester—come from the American Pregnancy Association website (http://americanpregnancy.org/), under the search 'fetal development first trimester' and 'fetal development second trimester.' The epigraph for part three—the Third Trimester—comes from the website Family Doctor (https://familydoctor.org/). The epigraph for part four—Afterbirth—comes from the website of the National Health Service of the UK (http://www.nhs.uk).

ACKNOWLEDGEMENTS

This book wouldn't exist without the prompting of Catherine Mellinger, the visual artist whose gorgeous collages form an integral element of the work. I'm unendingly grateful to Catherine for her talent, generosity, and encouragement.

I'd also like to thank Melanie Gordon and Paul Swoger-Ruston, two artists with whom Catherine and I collaborated, creating a multidisciplinary treatment of *Deep Salt Water*. Melanie's macro photographs elicit the intricacies and intimacies of Catherine's collages; and Paul's compositions beautifully amplify the rhythms and themes in the book. Thanks to the women of *Room*—the literary journal that featured the collaboration—especially Chelene Knight, Meghan Bell, and Cara Lang. What a pleasure to work with these artists, moving away from the solitude of sitting at a desk, with a pen and a blank sheet of paper, for years at a time!

My gratitude goes toward my early readers, Julie Joosten and Aaron Tucker, who provided vital feedback at a stage when I felt vulnerable with this work. Simi Rowen, Keva Glynn, and Jennie Goode guided me with specific advice and general enthusiasm—both of which were indispensible.

And then there's the intrepid team at BookThug: publisher Jay MillAr, managing editor Hazel Millar, copyeditor Ruth Zuchter, typesetter/designer Kate Hargreaves (whose task was Herculean), and David Goldstein, my editor. My thanks, to them, takes the form of a celebratory cheer! David, you were my ideal editor: exacting, incisive, relentless—but always good-humoured. Through your wisdom and unwavering understanding of this project's essence—and the places where I strayed from that core—I transformed *Deep Salt Water* from a manuscript into a book. I'm honestly not sure that could've happened otherwise.

Finally, I'd like to acknowledge people close to me—people whom I love—who weren't thrilled about the non-fiction nature of this project, but who didn't stand in my way. I offer this book as a means of apology, and thanks.

PHOTO: MELANIE GORDON

A recipient of the Chalmers Arts Fellowship and a KM Hunter Award Nominee, **MARIANNE APOSTOLIDES** is the author of six books, including three critically-acclaimed titles published by BookThug: *Swim, Voluptuous Pleasure* (listed among the Top 100 Books of 2012 by Toronto's *The Globe and Mail*), and *Sophrosyne*. Marianne lives in Toronto with her two children. Learn more on her website: marianne-apostolides.com.

CATHERINE MELLINGER is a mixed media and analog collage artist whose works find inspiration in the ideas originated by the feminist artists of the Dada period as well as the early Surrealists, lending to the exploration of dichotomy; real and unreal; beauty and trauma. Mellinger's works have been published in literary magazines, and she has been commissioned by musicians, writers and private collectors. She lives in Waterloo, Ontario, with her husband and son. To see more of her work, visit her website: www.cargocollective.com/catherinemellinger

Manufactured as the First Edition of
Deep Salt Water in the Spring of 2017
by BookThug.

Distributed in Canada by the Literary Press Group:
www.lpg.ca

Distributed in the US by Small Press Distribution:
www.spdbooks.org

Shop online at www.bookthug.ca

BOOK
PRODUCTION
WAR ECONOMY
STANDARD

Edited for the press by David Goldstein
Type + design by Kate Hargreaves
Copy edited by Ruth Zuchter